"Gives you insight into making your personal
commitment to climb your own mountain."
—Mark Suwyn, CEO and Chairman of the Board
of Louisiana Pacific, Inc.

"A clear, inspiring expression of the courage
it takes to balance commitments to others with
commitments to ourselves."
—Richard J. Leider, author of *Repacking Your Bags*

"Written from her own bedrock—Marilyn Mason's
'wise one' continues to amaze and to heal.
Goddess bless!"
—Olympia Dukakis,
Academy Award-winning actress

"Compassionate and wise."
—Harriet Lerner, Ph.D.,
author of *The Dance of Anger*

MARILYN MASON, PH.D., is also the author of *Making
Our Lives Our Own* and co-author of *Facing Shame*.
Clinical assistant professor at the University of
Minnesota and a corporate consultant, she lectures
nationally and internationally, and has appeared on *The
Ophra Winfrey Show*. As the director of Journeys Inward,
she has led groups in China, the Caucasus, Greece,
Africa, and Tibet. She lives in Minneapolis.

Seven Mountains

Life Lessons from a Climber's Journal

Marilyn Mason, Ph.D.

A PLUME BOOK

PLUME
Published by the Penguin Group
Penguin Putnam Inc., 375 Hudson Street, New York, New York 10014, U.S.A.
Penguin Books Ltd, 27 Wrights Lane, London W8 5TZ, England
Penguin Books Australia Ltd, Ringwood, Victoria, Australia
Penguin Books Canada Ltd, 10 Alcorn Avenue, Toronto, Ontario, Canada M4V 3B2
Penguin Books (N.Z.) Ltd, 182–190 Wairau Road, Auckland 10, New Zealand

Penguin Books Ltd, Registered Offices: Harmondsworth, Middlesex, England

Published by Plume, an imprint of Dutton NAL,
a member of Penguin Putnam Inc.
Previously published in a Dutton edition.

First Plume Printing, June, 1998
10 9 8 7 6 5 4 3 2 1

 REGISTERED TRADEMARK—MARCA REGISTRADA

The Library of Congress has catalogued the Dutton edition as follows:
Mason, Marilyn J.
    Seven mountains: the inner climb to commitment and caring /
Marilyn Mason.
        p.   cm.
    Includes bibliographical references.
    ISBN 0-525-93980-6 (hc.)
    ISBN 0-452-27417-6 (pbk.)
    1. Commitment (Psychology).   2. Caring.   I. Title.
BF619.M37   1997
158—dc20   96–41986
                                                       CIP

Printed in the United States of America
Original hardcover design by Leonard Telesca

BOOKS ARE AVAILABLE AT QUANTITY DISCOUNTS WHEN USED TO PROMOTE PRODUCTS
OR SERVICES. FOR INFORMATION PLEASE WRITE TO PREMIUM MARKETING DIVISION,
PENGUIN PUTNAM INC., 375 HUDSON STREET, NEW YORK, NEW YORK 10014.

For Morgan Elizabeth and all the children of the world—constant reminders of what commitment is all about.

Acknowledgments

No book is written alone. My list of companions along the way is long. Many friends read the earliest work. Ann Stefanson, Lois Braverman, Carrell Dammann, Deborah Boldt, Harriet Lerner, and Terence Williams were all there with solid feedback and support. Pamela Holt not only read but listened and so generously arranged the public reading of my work in progress. Sally Flax, Dick Leider, and Marilyn Peterson read each of the chapters and gave their diversely rich perspectives in honest feedback.

My loving family have always reminded me what commitment is about. In the very beginning my son, Jerry, and daughter-in-law, Lorrie, were there for the late-night commitment conversations. I am deeply grateful to my daughter, Jeanine, who was key to the shaping of these chapters. She was there at a critical time, giving invaluably honest feedback that only one who knows me so intimately can give. My sister, Sue, with her unwavering belief in me, has been there throughout, along with my brother-in-law, Don. I am blessed with their support.

For my friends through the decades I am eternally grateful. I am indebted to Sally and Jack Flax, who were constant in their belaying. Ethelyn and Howard Cohen once again gave loving support as well as stories to share. Constance Ahrons, constant colleague and dear friend, provided a steady stream of encouragement through fax, cartoons, and that special support only one who has been there can know. My deep appreciation to Iris, my dear friend, fellow colleague and traveler, who shares the spirit of adventure that continues to take us to facing new edges.

It is difficult to list all those who showed me the wilderness and helped me find my way. My wilderness teacher, Connie Hilliard, friend, belays as well off the rock as on. I am deeply grateful for the teaching from Will Steger, Annie Callaway, Dick Galland, Joe Baily, and all the gang from the early Wilderness Learning Institute. To Thad Peterson and the entire Dorobo family, including Koyie, I'll always be indebted for teaching me to love the Africa you love.

I have been blessed with good editorial folks. Kathleen Michels once again gave her sage editorial assistance. And David Milofsky, in his critical voice as a writer and teacher, came in toward the end with the art of differing with respect. No one could ask for better office support than I have in Lynn Ready—secretary and assistant, whose spirit of cooperation is a model for us all. I am grateful for her many talents.

This book has been born out of the spirit in places near and far. Special writing places were a part of it all: Marilyn Peterson and Norton Armour's lovely lake cabin, Rancho La Puerta, and Santa Fe were just a few.

I am grateful for the friendship of Rob Pasick, who introduced me to Ellen Levine, a literary agent extraordinaire. Ellen's dynamic bundle of competency and support has been unwavering. Ellen, in turn, led me to Michaela Hamilton, my spirited, adventurous editor who "got it" from the very beginning. Michaela constantly reminded me that a concept always interrupts an experience and that this was indeed my book.

My deepest gratitude goes to those who risked the inner climbs, whose stories are told here. Know that your courageous commitments can inspire others as you have me.

Contents

Introduction

Our lives are absorbed by our commitments, whether we choose them or not. We have commitments to our parents, to our loved ones, to our children, to our friends, and to our work. Yet amid the busyness of everyday life, with all its constant comings and goings, what these commitments really mean to us is often lost. Some we fulfill out of habit. Some are forced on us. Some we do for a short while, until a new and more interesting "commitment" comes up. At times it seems we are so absorbed in rushing through our lives, there is no one home when we look within. What does true commitment mean, anyway?

I had been caught in my own swirl of commitments. Then, quite by accident, I discovered a way to move beyond. In the great outdoors, at the base of a wild, untamed peak reaching to the sky, a very different spirit took hold. In climbing mountains, I found ways to overcome obstacles within myself. I learned how to make new commitments and redefine old ones—with real value to others and to myself.

It all began when I was on the medical school faculty at the University of Minnesota. It was the 1970s, a time alive with alternative education. A colleague, Skip Hofstrand, asked me to be the "psychological person" in teaching medical residents rock climbing. The goal was to help develop their expression of feelings. I was neither an outdoorswoman nor an athlete, but I said yes to the adventurous idea. When I went on that introductory climbing weekend, on Minnesota's North Shore of Lake Superior, to learn rock climbing and work with the residents, I had no idea that my major "work" would be with me!

The challenge wasn't just the physical act of scaling up the rock face. I did not expect the climb to be without difficulty, but I was not prepared for the revelation I experienced. On the rock face I was fully exposed, both outwardly and inwardly. Climbing soon became the catalyst for an "inner climb" that I encountered through my physical efforts.

Climbing became my metaphor for knowing commitment in a fresh, meaningful way. The concrete experiences of rock climbing transformed the meaning of commitment for me. I had lived a life in which commitment had meant dutifully fulfilling obligations. Rock climbing has taught me that commitment is not a static but rather a dynamic, alive process!

What's more, I learned that commitment starts at home. I had never asked the question: "Am I committed to me?" This was so new, I felt its naked rawness. As I exerted myself on the rocks, I often drew on focused energy and strength from previously unknown resources. I was surprised to learn what my body could do. Beyond that, rock climbing uncovered stored feelings, dormant strengths, failings, and unmet truths that I had buried.

After I had more experience, a small group of us formed a climbing company and began taking groups of couples, families, and business groups to the North Shore of Lake Superior and the Black Hills. I became increasingly excited as I saw people discover what I call the "wilderness within." I branched out to form an adventure psychology company in which we took rock climbing, rafting, backpacking, cross-country skiing, dogsledding, bicycling, canoeing, and trekking trips. We traveled throughout the United States and then took groups abroad. Around evening campfires we shared our daily discoveries and translated the metaphors of the day for use in our lives.

Eventually my travels took me to Tibet with my dear friend and colleague, Iris, a fellow trekker. I had wanted to explore the possibility of taking a group there. The Tibetans' reputation as the most religious people in the world influenced us strongly. Prayer life is not limited to the monasteries. Even in our first drive through the outskirts of Lhasa, we saw people turning their prayer wheels to accumulate merit, and burning juniper, its smoke carrying prayer to the gods.

I became aware of how pervasive spirituality is in the ancient Tibetan culture. Although cruelly oppressed by the Chinese, many Tibetans seemed to be fully committed to their spiritual life, their families, and one another. The scenes in Tibet were a dramatic contrast to my homeland, where it seems constant stimulation pulls me away from my self and my spirituality.

We headed toward Mt. Everest across the Tibetan Plateau. It has a unique beauty. Fierce winds and ice have created a brown-gray scree, mixed with vistas of fine sand, often colored a deep mauve under the late afternoon sun. Dried shrubs cling for survival as tenaciously as the prayer flags we constantly viewed as we crossed the plateau.

On our arrival at the Mt. Everest Base Camp, we learned that the Tibetans there bathe once a year. I smiled as I thought about home, where it seems we bathe constantly and *pray* once a year! When I wrote my journal entries, I felt I had been handed a new lens with the message "Now look at life through this."

Tibet reminded me that at one time I had lived my commitments almost as automatically as did the Tibetans. Like so many others of my day, I had done what my culture taught me to do—seldom questioning, living out my duty-bound role prescriptions in what I now call "role sleep." I realized I did not have an honest model of commitment that fits my life today. And I knew I wasn't alone. I came to a decision that a major life principle was not in place for me.

Commitment is in crisis in the United States. The pendulum has swung from one extreme—an ethos of self-sacrifice of the 1950s—to the opposite extreme—the self-indulgence of the 1980s, the "decade of excess." In a recent conversation one friend said teasingly, "Commit? Sure, at least till lunchtime!" Another remarked, "Commitment? But it's hard and it takes a long time!"

Recently I was invited to a seminar entitled "Mutually Uncommitted: The New Work Relationship." The title hit hard. Then I noted the following:

- In 1994, Manpower Temporaries became the largest private employer in the United States, hiring 640,000 Americans on a *temporary* basis! The number of people working for temporary employment agencies has grown by more than 240 percent.
- Young professionals will have three careers in a lifetime.
- Divorce is normal. Fifty percent of first marriages and 60 percent of second marriages end in divorce.
- Divorce for "starter marriages," marriages in the 25- to 29-year-old age group that are named after "starter homes," increased fivefold from 1962 to 1991. During that period the population for that age group didn't even double.
- Thirty percent of Americans now switch religions within their lifetime.

I could go on. The point is, we are living with rampant societal changes. Unlike in Tibet, immediate gratification has become the norm for many in our consumer culture. Everybody is in a hurry. Only in rare, fleeting moments do we wonder if we're running from ourselves. In a land of technological immediacy and intensity, what has happened to commitment?

In my consulting and therapy practice I see people daily struggling with their commitments to work, love, and family. Through the social changes of recent decades I have seen clients and friends who adopted choice and personal growth as part of their daily lives. When I began thinking about this book, my working title was, "Crucial Choices— How Do You Know When to Get Out—or Stay In?"

Climbing has taught me that commitment is a process, an inner climb of the mountains of the mind. My first inner climb was to face my fears—fear of failing, fear of vulnerability, and fear of not trusting my inner strength. The second climb was about trust—trust in my equipment, trust in my climbing partner, my belayer, and most of all, in myself. The third mountain of my inner climb was support and recognizing how essential it is for anchoring commitments. I learned that endurance—my fourth inner climb—was inherent in any climb, any commitment. I had learned that lesson well in meeting my family commitments, so it came easily. My next "climb," however, was more challenging: What did I do when I faced the crux of the climb—the decision point when I had to risk the unknown or down-climb? After the crux, I faced my sixth climb: to renew my contract or to down-climb. My seventh inner climb concerned my awareness of the spirit in commitment—the bedrock place within.

Through rock climbing I have learned how to make commitments more honestly from my heart, my own core values. Most important, I have learned a new ethos of commitment that allows me to balance my commitment to others with commitment to myself.

Come take a journey with me to seven mountains. We will look at some lessons learned on those slopes, both by myself and by fellow climbers. We will look at stories closer to home, of obstacles faced and overcome by people in everyday life. Commitments don't have to be chains. They can be rich with meaning. They can be the wings on which our spirits soar.

Chapter 1

Commitment: The Inner Climb

"Sometimes you search and search for the mountain without finding it until the time comes when you are sufficiently motivated and prepared to find a way through, first to the base, then to the summit."

—Jon Kabat-Zinn

THE NORTH SHORE, LAKE SUPERIOR. *Today was exciting—and terrifying. My directions had been simple—rappel down the cliff at Shovel Point and then climb back up. My legs were trembling with fear as I stood at the cliff edge over icy, deep Lake Superior. I knew immediately why climbers have coined the term "sewing machine legs."—rope knots secure on the carabiners (or rings), helmet fastened, and boot laces double-knotted. Yet as I stood on a cliff high over the water, all my feelings of security transformed into fears. How could this be? After all the experiences of the past two days of belaying, climbing, and rappelling, I thought I'd be somewhat confident here at the lake's edge.*

Waves of fear overtook me, like a young child's crayon strokes erratically filling the space within the lines. I froze. I dropped to my knees and slowly crawled over to the edge. My companions let me find my own way; no one laughed or commented. They just waited. All my energy drained from my arms; I was grateful to feel my knees on the small crushed stones that crusted the edge. As I watched my friend Jim standing confidently near the cliff's edge, I told myself that this was absolutely the only time I would ever do this to myself. I was too fearful even to feel embarrassed. Gradually I was able to feel my breathing. I remembered my friend's advice about exhaling deeply to relax my muscles and gain more steadiness. I exhaled steadily and felt life restored in my arms. I felt my limbs supporting me. I arose and slowly stood on both feet.

Dan, my thirty-seven-year-old belayer, was to protect me from falling by keeping the ropes under control so that he could arrest any fall at any time. He was relaxed—the stately, steady posture that only years of successful experience can give. I totally trusted him. Jim said, in his "of course you can" voice, "Okay, Marilyn, you're ready to rappel."

Now it was up to me to walk just five feet to the cliff's edge. Again I froze. More shaking, more tears. Then Jim asked, "Are you afraid of the height?" I nodded. "Yes, but it's not just that." "Are you afraid to let go?" he asked. I shook my head. "Are you afraid Dan won't hold you if you should fall?" he asked steadily. "I don't fear that at all," I wept. "Just what are your tears, Marilyn?" he gently asked. Suddenly I heard my voice unexpectedly stating, "I'm afraid of not achieving—not making it!" Surprise struck us all. Just where did that come from? I don't think I had ever thought of myself as an achiever—or a nonachiever either. This felt so foreign to me, yet by saying it I was relieved.

I stepped back off the edge and began to rappel. In the process I felt myself relaxing. I enjoyed the thrill, the exhilaration of rappelling as gravity carried me down. It was so easy that I felt like a bit of a show-off in my sense of newfound freedom. I bounced my feet lightly against the rock wall as I lowered myself, just as I had seen on television. (I had not yet learned that "bouncing" down is against the ethics of climbing and is hard on the ropes.) Still, I felt confident now and even released one hand from my belay rope so that I could wave up to Jim.

Finally, I felt my feet touch a ledge—a small shelf of rock where I was to untie my rappel rope and begin climbing. Awkwardly I unclipped my carabiners from my rappel rope and winced as I saw it *fall to my side. I saw why they called the rope "the umbilical." It was truly a lifeline between Dan and me at that moment. My life was in his hands.*

I called up, "Climbing!" Dan replied with the usual code, "Climb!" I stayed focused and slowly, clumsily, began to make my way up. Then I reached a point of "impossibility." I could see no handholds or footholds between where I stood and the small rock handhold to the left high above me. After taking too long trying to figure it out, and knowing fully the power of "I can't," I felt some energy emerge from some mysterious place within. I took a deep breath and leapt for the far-off hold. I then saw a fresh approach—a wholly new view of the rock—from this perspective. I saw different handholds and footholds; the route held new possibilities. My fears transformed into excitement. I felt drunk with exhilaration. I continued slowly up the rock face, feeling my connection with Dan through the taut rope and his occasional gentle tugs, reminding me I was safe. The fear had left; something deep and powerful took its place.

When I reached the top, I untied and fell into friends' and Dan's arms. I was flooded with tears, joy, and most of all, dazzling awareness. I was limp and exhausted, yet filled with energy. Never had I learned so much, so quickly, so graphically. I was deeply struck with the psychological "blitz" of climbing.

As a psychotherapist who relied heavily on talk, I viscerally learned that my body does not lie; my nonverbal behavior, visible to all, was indelibly truthful. Most dramatically, the rock made me confront myself. The rock face shuns ambiguity and demands honesty. While the physical risking was challenging, my climbing experience clarified who I was in my life.

At that time, though, I had no idea that I was seeking clarity. My life was full, at times overflowing. Along with my private practice as a therapist and my position on the faculty at the University of Minnesota, I was completing my doctorate. I had been shaping my professional identity as well as reshaping my identity as a single woman after a divorce from a twenty-year marriage. I certainly was in no need of new experiences.

The climbing weekend was the origin of what was to become an evolving metaphor that would shape my life. Yet my North Shore initiation had begun accidentally. A physician friend and fellow faculty member, Tad, an experienced climber, age forty-two, had invited me to join him and his friends to teach medical students to rock climb. I laughingly replied, "Who, me?"

Tad, a confident leader, believed that physicians are cognitively overdeveloped and emotionally underdeveloped, and he wanted to focus on what we called in the medical school "affective development." Today we refer to this as balancing E.Q. (emotional quotient) scores, which Dan Goleman wrote about, with high I.Q. scores.

In that initial weekend, we spent two full days learning basic rock craft, which included learning to use the equipment—helmets, ropes, and carabiners. Our initial climbs were in a secure, birch tree clearing on inland rocks at the base of Minnesota's highest "peak"—far from the water's edge.

Tad's desire to awaken emotion was rewarded almost immediately. Along with the medical residents, I discovered that "body truth"—the dormant feelings, strengths, and vulnerabilities buried unconsciously in the body—can be exposed through powerful nonverbal experiences. I recalled my graduate school training in nonverbal communication: Body language is five times more believable than verbal.

The first challenge was confronting my trust in myself. After a few practice runs, I began politely suggesting that others should climb first, secretly hoping that we would run out of time. No such luck. Up I'd go—to confront myself. I learned what I did when I was stuck, frozen in fear, and how I attempted to cover these fears. I became acutely aware of when I wanted to cheat, of when I felt powerless and helpless. Though I found I can be pretty tenacious, I also began to learn the importance of down-climbing, or knowing when to back down when a situation is impossible—or when I'm not ready.

These initial lessons were not only directed inwardly, though. I also learned, most reluctantly, how to ask for support. My initial climb with my partner, Dan, revealed a parallel with commitment—it was between us, mutual, and filled with energy. Dan's voice still rings in my ears: "Remember, you're committed to the climb!" I had been stuck, but after this vote of support, I began to breathe deeply, repositioned myself, and climbed quite smoothly.

This process was helped by the fact that I felt a strong compassionate connection with climbers as they struggled. When they were stuck, my muscles tightened. When they made progress, I breathed deeply and felt joy with them. When they completed a climb and untied from their ropes, I always sighed, feeling that I too had climbed—at least emotionally.

I was immediately intrigued. After the first two days, we talked at night in the cabin about what we had learned.

Bob and Shelly, both young medical residents, struggled with his constant control of her; he always wanted to save her from any hurt or fears. When she had been stuck on her climb, Bob felt painfully helpless as he discovered he was feeling her pain. Allowing himself to cry, he said he realized that in this graphic "letting go" lesson, Shelly did not need him to protect her.

Gary, a forty-one-year-old psychiatry student, had discovered that he tended to turn to the future and worry or to look back and regret. On the rock, he said, "I have been missing what is here in front of me—all the obvious support, the handholds and footholds, available to me if I stay in the present." He added, "I learned more in two days on the rock than I did in two and a half years in psychotherapy!" Even my adolescent son, on his first climbing trip, had an insight: "Mom, we're all equal on the rock."

On the North Shore trip, I began to question my commitments. I had known little about what I truly cared about and wanted from life beyond my prescribed expectations. For many years commitment had meant promises sealed with endurance, driven by blind loyalty. My commitments were all outer-directed, toward others' expectations—in marriage, children, family of origin, friends, and organizations. To have seriously considered myself then would have meant that I was selfish. I recall how shocked my children were to learn that they too were part of this equation—that my husband and I had never sat down and thought about *choosing* to be parents. "You were the commitment that followed marriage," I stated honestly. Back then I couldn't have lived differently; I did not really know who I was. My commitments had seemed to bypass any deep reflection or conscious choices. I was what we now refer to as a fifties woman.

My first climb showed me something totally new, and totally raw; it taught me, or rather forced me, to stay with myself. It was on the mountain when I began to see that climbing was about my commitment to me.

The Beginning of a Journey

I had never considered the idea of being committed to me, to my own truth. I had seldom asked, "Does this come from what *I* know to be true?" My friend Harriet Lerner asked, "Do you realize how unique it is to be committed to self-truth?" She is right; it is unique to find our own truth and then stay with it.

My self-truth intensified with commitment upheavals that took place in those rousing years of the sixties and seventies. That era of social change, consciousness raising, and active, passionate involvement in peace and justice issues was still alive when I returned to the university to complete my degrees. I questioned everything in those years and felt support of newfound friends. The civil rights movement, human rights movement, Nietzsche's "God is dead" assumption, the sexual revolution, the Vietnam War, and feminism punctured my balloons of neatly fixed beliefs. Now I know they were not my own chosen beliefs.

I joined the choir of protest. Scores of my friends, students, and clients also made dramatic life changes based on our "need to grow" in our relationships. I, like so many others, faced moral and ethical dilemmas as I realized my ethical ideals had been denied, betrayed, or sacrificed. "Forevermore" seemed like a cultural antonym in contrast to the exciting message "Be here now." For the first time in my life I felt I had permission to leave any commitment in the name of "personal growth." Books such as *Creative Divorce* reflected our changing attitudes toward divorce.

I began to agonize about whether to leave my long-term marriage. I did what so many of my friends had done in the early 1970s. I saw an attorney rather than a therapist. I had been discovering my own voice—and it was very different from the voice of a woman fresh out of college. Differences in politics, religion, and economics were weighing heavily on the "let's avoid these" shelf. Morally and ethically, I felt troubled and ambivalent about my decision to explore leaving my thirteen-year marriage. My struggle became a secret I shared with only one friend. The attorney, hearing my story about our college-sweetheart start and our two young children, reminded me of my commitment and, in essence, told me to go home and be a good wife.

My sentimentality, ambivalence, and years of trained deference rallied to his command. I promptly blamed myself and told myself that I wasn't working hard enough at my marriage. Actually, I was even somewhat relieved. After all, when we had married in the fifties, "until death do us part" meant forevermore. I had vowed to stay, no matter what. Still, I tucked the possibility of leaving into that reservoir of the mind that holds the seeds of all possibilities. I resolved not to attend any more personal growth workshops. "Put this personal growth on hold; it's hurting our marriage," I told myself. Surely personal growth can be a part of a marriage, yet it had not been a part of our marital philosophy. I discovered strong values differences, and I couldn't erase my new discoveries. Newfound aspects of me would not disappear.

I continued to struggle, anchored by two prevailing thoughts: not hurting two children who mattered so much and upholding my family's pride about the fact that no Mason woman had ever divorced. My husband and I even built a new home, acting on that desperate cliché to do anything we could to save our marriage. After seven more years, filled with denied feelings, rationalizations, and a deep sense of knowing and heavy guilt, I asked for a divorce.

My divorce was a marker of my self-commitment. Most of my education had taught me to believe, not to think. My beliefs in my highly institutionalized commitments, along with all their social expectations, were crumbling. I saw that I had made many decisions by default. As I divorced, I knew painfully there would be consequences for others. I was also committed to me, to my own truth.

With my divorce I was suddenly financially responsible for my own life. My income from my new teaching position had been our "extra" income. With no-fault divorce and limited financial support, I tumbled headlong into deep fears. Today I chuckle when younger people ask, "What motivated you in your adult life?" My response has always been the same: terror. Risk-taking continued to feel easier after that major decision and the painful period that followed. I had started on a fresh route. My fifties ethic held vestiges of my true values, but I reexamined my obligations.

Once I was free of the hidebound commitment to marriage, I looked around and saw a rapidly changing society in which commitment seemed to matter less and less. The social activism of the sixties was settling into the Me Decade. Just how was I to live my life? I now knew how to end a commitment, and I knew I would not want to live my life only for me. Yet what else had I learned about commitment? I was confused.

The Cultural Dermapatch

I remember a conference in Copenhagen, where family sociologists, psychotherapists, and social workers representing thirty nations gathered to share our experience of working with families. The convener interrupted the din of excited voices. She began speaking slowly, deliberately, "Welcome to Copenhagen, where our caring is public." I was stunned; her words connected with something deep within me. What had I heard in those eight words?

The Danish woman's pride had tapped my pain. I knew my pain was shame—my own internalized shame. I thought about *our* nation's "public caring": food stamps, AFDC, and humiliatingly long lines for welfare payments. What a contrast to her statement was the one I have often used when I open my workshops: "We live in a shame-bound, sexist, racist, classist, ageist, homophobic, addictive culture, and we're in it together." Yevgeny Yevtushenko, the Russian poet, said that shame is the most powerful motivator of human progress. As I thought about how our society values economic success as the measure of worth, I asked myself, "Just what are we committed to?"

I thought about Dermapatches—those Band-Aid–type patches that are taped to the skin to medicate—to prevent seasickness or stop smoking. Dermapatches, with their continuous low-grade doses, work so gradually that we often forget we are wearing them. Our culture acts on us in the same way, involuntarily seeping into our psyches, imprinting our brains with cultural messages. How many of us have been seduced by subliminal or explicit messages that promise us financial success, beauty, thinness, sophistication, belonging, or feeling good?

I was reminded of a trip to Ellis Island with a friend whose family had come through there from Europe. As we wandered through the Great Hall, we sat in the same places where the immigrants had sat and looked at the buildings that housed those who were to be sent back to their homelands because of diseases or lack of funds. As we sat there, I was filled with overwhelming admiration for the courage it took to leave a homeland, often at a young age, and arrive here with the twenty-five dollars necessary to be allowed entry to this country. We took the same tests the immigrants took and saw the many vestiges of the homeland cultures of these new Americans. We saw shoes, clothing, books, and even a few toys. At day's end, we returned to the ferry boat filled with people of diverse languages and skin colors. The melting pot of Ellis Island was alive and well today.

From the immigrant experience, though, our nation has now become a rich and troubled cultural amalgam with no shared cultural heritage.

I had a moment of clarity. We are a nation of cutoffs, divorced from deep cultural roots. I began to feel a new-found compassion for our complex identity. I had been concerned for some time that my natural capacity for compassion, so present with my clients, families, and friends, seemed absent in my social activism. I had been committed to taking public stands and had felt the empowerment of civil disobedience and going to jail. I carried my mother's voice of indignation: "That will not do!"

Anger was a driving force for many activists, and it had deepened our drive to create change. It took me a while to realize that my anger totally blocked my compassion and understanding. This problem had only worsened because no legislative action ever seemed enough for deep and lasting change.

At this point, what I called my healthy skepticism about social change was now edging on cynicism. I wondered whether I had moved so far beyond the naiveté of my youth that I had lost something vital. Shortly after the Ellis Island visit, I was invited to address the annual meeting of the managing editors of the Associated Press. Awaiting my time to speak, I looked out at an audience of several hundred managing editors, mostly male, from all parts of the United States. As their leader scanned the room from our banquet table, he said, "You have before you the most cynical group of Americans ever assembled." I had a sinking feeling; these managing editors were the shapers of the daily information that fills our lives.

How different this was from a society I know in Africa. Robin and Thad are a naturalist couple who live in a family community, sharing the responsibilities of child care, farming, and conducting safaris. They live their commitments consciously in work, friendship, family, and community. One morning, before leaving for a safari, the brothers and wives made a series of calls to one another. It was the anniversary of the death of their brother's child, who had died shortly after birth the year before. Somehow they knew naturally how to grieve, how to connect with one another. Deeply struck by their natural caring, I referred to it over tea one day. I said, "Do you realize what you have here?" Robin immediately replied, "Yes, we do." Then, after a pause, she added, "We know it's natural; it's just not normal."

Robin's statement struck me. I find that most people do care deeply and do want to make responsible, conscious choices, despite the negative rhetoric of Christopher Lasch and his ilk who argue that Americans are not committed to future posterity, that we lack commitment. I also realized that most people do commit, often unconsciously, on a regular basis, even though they may deny it. They simply do not have conscious commitments that matter to them. As a result, it is easy to bash ourselves, saying that we Americans either don't know how to commit or that we commit only to cultural imperatives.

In thinking about committed lives, I thought of Martin Luther King, Jr., Daniel Berrigan, Mother Teresa, Gandhi, and Nelson Mandela. I thought of Johnetta Cole, who has dedicated her adult life to educating young black people. I thought about MADD (Mothers Against Drunk Driving) and how it began when one woman's commitment mushroomed into changing our nation's drunk-driving laws.

Then I recalled many neighbors, friends, and relatives who quietly live their commitments intentionally through their jobs or careers as well as through unpaid work. I know a 101-year-old Greek man who has cared for our office building's garden for the past thirty-five years, working on bended knee, smiling at the flowers he tends. I have numerous friends committing to caring for their elderly parents. Then I thought of the towering total of volunteer hours people commit to each day, thereby increasing our social capital and sustaining all our institutions. The list reminded me how natural it is to commit and how much life matters when we are committed to something we truly care about.

Given that we live in a nation replete with choices, I think that many of us find it difficult to make conscious commitments. In this immediate and ever changing culture, the very word commitment can seem antiquated. Commitment comes from the Latin root word *mittere*, which means "to send." This implies that we give ourselves in commitment; we "send" our word into another. This root word implies action, yet I don't think it meant action to most of us as we grew up.

Commitment in Crisis

When I received an invitation to a seminar entitled "Mutually Uncommitted: The New Work Relationship?" I felt clear about what was happening. Commitment is in crisis. Immediacy, disposability, and a changing economy have changed our culture dramatically. I just received a call from the *Wall Street Journal* regarding the effects of work on the family. The reporter had heard some stories about young children, in their Barbie and Ken dialogues, asserting, "I'm downsizing you, Ken," to which Ken replies, "I'm out-placing you." We talked about this as an example of how the changing work world has entered the home.

I saw that the ethos of commitment has swung from one extreme—self-sacrifice and forevermore of the 1950s—to the opposite extreme—the self-indulgent "decade of excess" of the 1980s. Before my son's wedding, he said with deep concern, "Mom, I can't think of marriage without thinking of divorce! You and Dad didn't marry in a world with such high divorce rates." He knew he did not want to divorce. At first I was baffled. What did he mean? What did this say about commitment? Would this be a "temporary" marriage? How much had society changed? How far had the pendulum of commitment swung?

As I thought more deeply about his remark, I decided his attitude was realistic given that half of today's marriages will likely end in divorce. Commitment no longer means forevermore—no matter the cost—as it had in previous decades. These soon-to-be newlyweds were not about to commit themselves blindly to a protective institutional umbrella as we had. Rather, they seemed to be committed not only to each other but also to their own individual growth within their marriage. They carefully examined their core values, exploring similarities and differences. They were wide awake about marriage, and knew that marriage means consciously working at it.

Somewhere between the "forevermore" blind institutional loyalty of the past—the traditional meaning of commitment—and the self-indulgent "for this moment" attitude is a balanced center. In my adult struggles, I had never thought about balancing my serious investment in those I cared for with my commitment to my own core values. I now see this new ethos of commitment as a scale with a supportive fulcrum balancing both sides of commitment. We will always have moral responsibilities to others, but we also need commitments of passion—in causes, the arts, athletics, or politics—to nurture our souls.

Commitment is dynamic. Even in our obligatory family commitments, we can see an unfolding process. We do it ourselves, but we don't do it alone.

I'll always remember fondly the eighty-five-year-old widow who learned in therapy that her elder son was gay. She returned weekly with both of her sons to work through other family secrets. They were all committed to being together in therapy. One day, after her third visit, as she struggled on the stairway because of her stiff legs, I asked her why she kept coming back. I said, "You can get away with anything at your age, you know." She turned to me and stated emphatically with crisp indignation, "Well, I care, don't I?" I smiled back knowingly. She somehow knew that it is never too late. Many months later, her sons called to tell me their mother had died. She had been completely surrounded and held by all her family members, who could now show their caring. Such caring is intrinsic to our nature and fosters spirited, conscious commitments.

Spirited Life Climbs

I think back to my climb on Lake Superior's north shore and recall what it taught me about my facing my *fear*—of falling, of failing, of shame. My outer climbs summoned my inner climb. As I met the unknown through these intense, dramatic experiences, I saw how pragmatic the metaphor was in my daily life. Again and again I learned that the greatest mountain I will ever climb is inside me. These "climbs" awakened my consciousness and became my map for all my commitments—to myself as well as to others. Climbing became my touchstone.

Rene Daumal, my favorite French philosopher and author of *Mt. Analogue: A Non-Euclidean Adventure in Mountain Climbing*, said it clearly:

> For a mountain to play the role of Mt. Analogue, its summit must be inaccessible, but its base accessible to human beings as nature has made them. It must be unique, and it must exist geographically. The door to the invisible must be visible.

The doors are different for each of us. A neighborhood center in the Bronx can hold challenges equal to those of a sheer rock wall on Lake Superior. Diving into a foxhole in Vietnam, coping in cities torn apart by drug epidemics, facing chronic illness, struggling in a relationship after a secret is divulged, or seeking alcoholism treatment are all climbs. I learned that adventure is an attitude—an attitude about a process—that transforms an experience.

In a world filled with choice, commitment also implies risk. Risk is fickle; one person's comfort is another's moment of terror. The Outward Bound staff who worked with me on climbing trips were sensitive, gentle, strong men and women who moved about on the rocks as nimbly as mountain sheep. The rest of the climbers and I felt awed by their ability to climb so comfortably, their vertical dance. In those early days when I reminded the staff about our evening group meeting to tell the day's stories, they looked aghast. "You don't mean we have to sit in a circle and talk about it, do you?" several asked. For them, sharing their feelings in a group was *their* risk. They felt as vulnerable taking emotional risks as we did taking physical risks.

Our conscious commitments do not come from mastering any great world peak or reaching any end point. Conscious commitments are born out of our journey of spirit, our inner climbs. These inner climbs lead us to living our lives with meaning and to becoming more of who we are.

Chapter 2

Fear: Facing Our Edges

"What difference do it make if the thing you scared of is
real or not?"
—Toni Morrison

THE ANNAPURNA REGION, THE HIMALAYAS, NEPAL.
*Tonight we have camped in one of the natural beds so characteristic
of the Himalayas—a stone-sprinkled, grassy mountainside with cor-
rugated furrows just wide enough and deep enough to hold a few
tents. I have tied my Tibetan chimes onto the outside of my backpack. I have carefully arranged the two three-inch disks close to each
other. If anyone touches my backpack, the chimes, in strong, vibrant
reverberations, will awaken me and hinder any invader. I feel almost
smug with my new security system, yet a shadow of fear still hovers
over me—probably left over from today's climbing.*

*Today's climbing had terrified me when my trek turned into a
climb. In the friendly Himalayan countryside, I felt relaxed when
Sherpa Norpu and I began trekking. After trail lunch with some
trekkers from France, we resumed hiking. Quite suddenly the trails
narrowed. I felt my mouth becoming dry and my hands sweaty as I
grasped my walking stick more tightly. Then I looked down and I
shuddered. This vista of beauty became a landscape of fear.*

*I slowed my pace; my fear distanced me from Norpu. I focused
on breathing, yet my entire upper body tightly resisted. Norpu, in
the lead, beckoned me from a high ridge. "Come, madam, this is a
shortcut." I looked up at a steep, bare rock face and froze in place.*

"Let's just take the long route," I pleaded. "I am sorry, madam, but we would be hiking in the dark, and you know there have been bandits. Come this way; I am here."

Yet Norpu might as well not have been there. I could not feel his typically reassuring presence. I felt alone in the world as I faced the long rock face before me.

I took the first steps up the face, and as my right foot slid on small pea-size stones, I clutched a rock above me. It too slid away. My legs were shaking. I began talking to my feet. I told myself to stand tall and straight away from the rock, yet my fear bent me forward in a precarious position. I tried to wrench my shoulders away from the rock. I swore in anger. Waves of loneliness swept over me. I heard Norpu's voice trailing in the wind, yet could not understand his message. Suddenly, as if out of nowhere, I saw a small rock platform above. I stretched my leg up and over the ledge and miraculously stood with "three points on"—with both my arms stretched out to give balance to my single-footed position. Feeling somewhat secure in my newfound position, I could breathe and reposition myself.

Now I could clearly hear Norpu's voice. "Madam, madam, I am here; do not be afraid." I was irritated at being told not to feel what I was feeling. "Why doesn't he know better?" I groused to myself. I needed empathy, not advice. I winced as I recalled how often I had done that same thing when attempting to be helpful. I made a silent promise to be more mindful when encouraging others back home.

I knew not to linger long; I continued climbing, yet my confidence seemed to take a roller-coaster ride. As I neared the top, I saw Norpu's smiling face beaming down at me. "Good, madam. Yes, madam," he called out. On top, I lay down on my back, exhausted, as if to refill my security from the solid horizontal rock.

Facing fear was my first inner climb to commitment. Often deeply buried, often unknown, our fears are a major obstacle to commitment.

The Himalayas confronted me with a concert of fears, stemming from my fear of falling, my fear of being hurt.

These fears were primal, stemming from deep in the psyche. Yet many of the fears—either in our private lives or in our careers—that hold people back today have equally deep roots, often dating to injuries in childhood. We can't get beyond them, because we have hidden them so well from ourselves. What is needed is the willingness to uncover these fears, to face them so that they can be put behind us or transformed into courage. When this happens, our energy becomes unblocked, enabling our lives to become more free.

I've certainly known fears less exotic than one of plunging into a thousand-foot chasm. When my door to fear opens in any present experience, fears from the past rush in and flood me. It seems as if they wait behind the swinging door to my psyche, bursting forth most unpredictably.

Years ago I was in a car accident in which I was severely hurt, and was told that I could go blind. Long after my eyesight had returned to normal and my injuries healed, I retained a residue of terror when traveling in cars. Initially it grabbed me so strongly that I would ride only in the backseat, often down on the floor. Even now it still flutter-kicks deep inside me from time to time when I ride with a lead-footed driver. While the fear is understandable, how could it remain so vivid more than forty years later?

Another good example of deeply rooted fear comes from a client of mine. In this case, unblocking fear came simply from recognizing it for what it was. In naming the problem, it can often be solved.

Timothy, a fifty-year-old corporate executive, was a compulsive and highly successful professional. He came to see me about his anxiety. He said he had been able to manage it through the years, but when he took international flights, now regularly part of his work, he thought he would die. "I'm weary from trying to hold on." Timothy had kept his anxiety a secret, telling no one except his wife, who later reported her weariness at being his sole listener.

In therapy, Timothy revealed that he was the son of two alcoholic parents. He described how many times he had anxiously sat on the stairway holding his younger sister's hand, awaiting his parents' return home at night. He waited fearfully, often for hours, wondering when and if they would return. "At age seven," he recalled, "I turned thirty."

As in rock climbing, the key to unblocking himself was in confronting his past. I asked Timothy to visit a grade-school playground and observe the lives of seven-year-olds. In our next session, he reported, "They laugh, they play!" "Yes, that's just what seven-year-olds are supposed to do," I reminded him. He continued, with a faraway look in his eyes, "And some of their parents are there to pick them up!"

Timothy discovered that the fearful, anxious boy he once was had been locked in a psychological closet for many years. He realized that his fear-filled childhood had greatly affected his adult life. "I think I've been held hostage all these years—by myself."

Realizing a part of him was frozen in time, Timothy became committed to embracing his fear. I showed him a quote from Arthur Miller's *After the Fall*: "I dreamed I had a child, and even in the dream I saw it was my life. And it was an idiot, and I ran away. But it always crept on to my lap again, clutched at my clothes until I thought, if I could kiss it, whatever in it was my own, perhaps I could sleep, and I bent to its broken face and it was horrible . . . but I kissed it. I think one must finally take one's life in one's arms, Quentin."

Timothy nodded, saying, "That's it, isn't it?" As he told his life story, he found buried pain—the loneliness of the cutoff feelings and his grief over the absence of a secure childhood. By sifting through family photographs he found a connection with the boy he once was and in empathy carried a photo of that seven-year-old in his pocket.

One day Timothy came to the session feeling very anxious. "I have to conduct a board meeting next week," he said in a dry, controlled voice. He had been feeling vulnerable and uncertain about the new, unfamiliar feelings that were surfacing as he revisited his past. I suggested that he not lock the child in the closet. Instead, he could let the anxious boy be symbolized by his left hand, and his competent adult self by his right hand as a reminder that he was still connected. Timothy reported back that he had conducted the meeting with his right hand holding his left hand under the table. He said, with a relaxed grin, that no one in the boardroom knew anything about his vulnerability. He had stayed with himself.

Timothy had learned vividly that if he took his fear with him, he could convert it into courage. He began to make dramatic changes in his relationships with all those around him as he gained respect and compassion for his history. Toward the end of his therapy, he suddenly recalled the story of the kidnapping of the Lindbergh child and Charles Lindbergh's flight across the ocean. Somehow his fear glued them together. In guided imagery he created another ending to the story. By the time Tim finished therapy, he was able to take international flights without anxiety. He also learned what it is to live a fully feeling life.

Many of us have been stuck as Timothy was—unknowingly held hostage to buried fears. Often we are unaware of the ways they become unconscious barriers to commitment, making us onlookers in our own lives.

Here's another case of long-buried fear that could not be resolved until it was faced. Charlene had never realized that she took her fear of abandonment into the workplace. A senior executive, she was committed to her career in marketing. She was well liked by her employees; she was always available. The cost of her availability, however, resulted in her falling behind in all her projects. Her door was always open; she had never thought of closing it! When discussing the meaning of this with me, Charlene related a story from her past.

As an overresponsible eleven-year-old in a blue-collar family, Charlene had wanted desperately to go to language camp. Her parents found the funds for it, and she was thrilled. When she returned home, though, feeling pleased with herself and excited about honors she had won, she faced a house of gloom. Her mother and father were divorcing; her father had already moved out. With the logic of a child, Charlene told herself that if she had stayed home, this might not have happened. She promised to herself to always stay present so that "bad things won't happen."

Charlene was stunned when she realized that her childhood fear of abandonment was being played out in her office on a daily basis. By revisiting the event that shaped that belief, she could let go of the fear and could close her office door. She could also hold on to her own "stuff," not give herself away, and move more deeply into commitment.

For many people, fear stems not only from inside themselves but from the lessons they learn from the society around them as well. This is most evident in people's careers. Despite the inroads made by the feminist revolution, archaic social values continue to shape the way men and women view their careers. The two halves of this could be called fear of failure and fear of success.

Fear of Failure

To illustrate this divergence in gender, I'll use an example from my own past. Some years ago, after both my children had left home, I moved to Santa Cruz, California, to accept a job as clinical director of a women's health program. I also accepted a part-time faculty job in the psychology department at the University of California, Santa Cruz. It was exciting to live on the ocean and have access to so much wilderness. I thought I had it all.

Soon, though, work at the clinic turned sour for me. I

discovered that my ethical standards seriously differed from those of the director. I learned that unknowing medical patients were being labeled chemically dependent in order to pad figures for additional grant funding from a project. I confronted the director, but nothing changed. I decided to leave. The head of the psychology department, who knew the clinic well, said he respected my decision to leave.

When I returned home to Minnesota to friends, family, and work, I was grateful to be back, but I was shocked when a few remarked, "Sorry it failed out there." They did not say that I failed, but they might as well have. After noting a few of these responses, I saw that many men outside my friend-ship circle viewed failure differently from women. Women friends said, "Good for you; you did not compromise your values. Welcome home." One man, on the other hand, asked, "What was it like to have to come back?" I was sur-prised by his question, as if returning meant failure. I had not considered it a failure. I had been disappointed, of course, but the clinic had not been right for me.

In my consulting practice, men speak openly with me about their fear of failure. For many, work means being a good provider, as their fathers were before them. When I was growing up in a middle-class WASP family, it would have been an insult to my father's dignity if my mother had worked outside our home in any other capacity than as a volunteer. It would have injured my father's dignity and would have meant failure to him. My mother, a former schoolteacher now a full-time mother and homemaker, knew one of her "jobs" was to protect him. Later in life, I saw that her status was truly a privilege and that the term "working woman" had a different meaning in many groups, including blue-collar families and many racial and ethnic minorities, where wives typically worked outside the home. This is not linked to dollars alone.

Success, most men have taught me, lies in power, money, and status. I have teased corporate clients about the male

PMS syndrome so common in corporations. Fear of failure drives competition. Gore Vidal said, "Each time a friend succeeds, I die a little." Others cover their fear of failure with "I don't care" or "I can't."

Not facing up to their fear of failure means that many people remain trapped. You can't climb a mountain when you're pretending it isn't there. Sometimes the question of failure depends on how you look at it in the first place, as can be seen in the case of one of my clients.

Mike, a sandy-haired, youthful, wiry man, was an honor student throughout his school years. After completing a master's degree, he decided that he wanted to teach high school English. His peers regarded him as highly successful in his field, and the students and community respected his creative teaching. But Mike never felt successful because academics' earning power is so much less than athletes'. He felt "lesser" than his two brothers, who were star professional athletes—one in baseball, the other in football.

Mike struggled with the meaning of success. When I asked him to define it, he could talk only about power. I asked him to write what success would look like. Mike discovered that even though it was not true for himself, he had swallowed the male myth of success having to do with titles, salary, and status.

Mike decided to raise the subject at a family reunion. To his surprise, he discovered that his brothers both felt that they were not successful because their success came from sports—that they hadn't made a "real" contribution to society as their teacher brother was doing. The brothers found they had opened a doorway to talking further about what success meant to them. Mike later admitted, "I am coming close now to getting over this fear of failure."

Both men and women have said that while they crave success, they also fear the cost. Fame is not the only thing that seduces us away from our true selves; it can arise from any position of power. I counsel many corporate people who talk about their loneliness at the top. As a result, these executives have begun to form support groups. Maybe the question each of us needs to ask is, "What is the cost of my success to my other commitments?"

Recently Dick Schlosberg, publisher and CEO of the *Los Angeles Times*, spoke at a corporate psychology meeting I attended. He recounted a meeting he had held with one of his top young male executives about a new project. In the midst of their meeting, at 4:45, the young man said, "Excuse me, I have to leave in five minutes. It's my day for day-care pickup." Schlosberg said he initially was stunned by his employee's behavior and then said he respected the young man for having taken such responsibility in the other areas of his life and not deferring to power. Schlosberg said, "We're going to have to get used to this." The meaning of success was changing in his office.

Maggie was the special one in her family. The first in her large African-American family to get a college education, she had become very successful in the business community and was highly respected in her professional and personal life. She held one of the few top positions in an insurance company. When Maggie's company brought in outside consultants, she was shocked to learn how negatively her peers and subordinates felt about her. At age fifty-two, she had never confronted her shadow side. "Why didn't this happen sooner?" she sputtered to friends. "Probably because you didn't want to tarnish your family's image of you; you wanted to be perfect," replied a good friend. Maggie realized the price she had paid for maintaining her image and plunged into the "work" she needed to do. When talking with her family members later, she learned that indeed their love was not conditional. Maggie had been governed by the belief that, if she was not as perfect as she could be, she would not be loved by her family or have a place there.

Fear of Success

On the other side of the coin, I hear more women than men talking about their fear of success. When I lecture on my book *Making Our Lives Our Own*, many single women remark, "I have been making my life my own, but now I'm afraid I'll be alone the rest of my life." I could not dismiss this; they were well aware that many people feel intimidated by highly successful women. Other women fear success because they know how it will affect their mates, husbands, and families.

Karen, a successful business executive, said she felt guilty when her salary almost tripled that of her husband, a school social worker. Fortunately, Don was comfortable enough to talk about his transient feelings of jealousy. Both knew that each was contributing a different kind of capital—hers financial, his social. They had several friends who lived with the same situation, so they had support for their financial differences.

Nancy, a petite and physically strong young woman, feared success in the business world. A successful physical therapist, she became interested in health care and sought her MBA degree. When she married, in the midst of her graduate studies, she became fearful. Both her mother and mother-in-law were traditional homemakers, and Nancy feared what they would think of her if she was successful in any other way than parenting. "On top of it all," she said, "I don't even know if I want any children." At family gatherings, Nancy withdrew, feeling she had nothing to say. She also felt lonely in her male-dominated field.

Nancy learned to work compulsively so she did not have to feel her fear. She moved ahead quickly. Her intense studies followed by an overwhelmingly responsible first job on Wall Street provided the structure for her fear. Nancy's guilt grew as her husband reminded her that he was entitled to more time. He said, "I want you to look at your fears—because that's what is driving you into your workaholism." Nancy's fear grew; she knew that if she slowed down, she would have to feel her fear of success.

Nancy joined a support group for women in management in which the initial issue the women discussed was their fear of success. Gradually, through talking openly about her fear, Nancy found she wasn't alone. During this time, her mother-in-law had written a card to her congratulating her on her recent promotion. "How proud of you we all are," she said. Nancy's eyes welled up with tears. "I never knew they would accept my choice," she said. "I thought they would see me as a failure if I stayed on my career track." In time, Nancy was able to make changes in her schedules and began to live a more balanced life.

Balance becomes a challenge for women who work both inside and outside the home. Lorrie, a married executive in a major New York firm, sees success for women existing at three levels: First is the professional or work level; the second is at the personal caregiving in relationships and the home environment; and the third is friendship and community. "Although you can compete with men on their grounds, you never have the same feeling," she said. "If you attain success at one level, your career, you immediately feel guilty because in the process you know you had to short-change two other dimensions of your life. So you don't really feel the success." Lorrie said that her field is dominated by men. She feels that she is an ambassador for women in the workplace since she is the only woman at her level. She feels a responsibility in that role. She said she is the only person in her group who does not have a stay-at-home wife. "There is an inherent tension in following the men and holding on to your values," she explained. "Also," she commented, "a high percentage of us out there had stay-at-home mothers and are without models for a working wife and mother."

She made the point that failure is different for women.

"When most women perceive failure, it is often because they realize they can't do all three."

Fear of Intimacy

When I asked my friend Penelope what her greatest fear was, she replied, "That's easy. Intimacy, of course!" The fear of intimacy is complex. It is the fear of connection—of vulnerability, of being seen, of being known, of being loved, of loss, and the fear of giving up one's myths about oneself.

My longtime friend Betsy said, "I am afraid of intimacy because I might be hurt." I replied, "Of course you will if what you have is real!" One of the most common phrases I hear in my practice is, "I can't say that; it would hurt him or her." I respond, "Have you ever been in a genuinely loving relationship of any kind that did not have some hurt in it?" Because we have a right to express our own feelings honestly, we do hurt our loved ones, often unknowingly and, also at times, intentionally.

One of the myths I discarded was the belief that a relationship guarantees intimacy. I learned that this simply is not true. Through establishing my life after divorce, I learned that being married does not guarantee intimacy any more than being single ensures loneliness.

Some years ago I defined intimacy as a shared experience of closeness and connection in a variety of activities that are deep and personal. These connections can occur in many contexts: social, emotional, intellectual, physical, recreational, affectional, sexual, aesthetic, and spiritual. In intimate relationships we expect that we not only will share in many of the areas, but that the relationship will continue over time.

When I include "deep and personal" in my definition, I am referring to connections developed through heated conflict as well as through tenderness. Too often people cheat themselves by thinking intimacy can be defined only as cozy, soft, and warm, or sexual. Intimacy also involves good, fair fighting.

Expressing feelings is great fuel for intimacy. Yet I have felt concern during the past decades when people make this the sole standard for intimacy. This is not true. We can know true feelings through energy conveyed, and this may or may not come with words. It can come through chopping wood together, gardening together, or sitting quietly.

Many problems of intimacy are gender-based, although this divide is lessening as time goes on. Still, an identifiable pattern remains. As dead as it may seem, the patriarchal system still lives on in the attitudes of men and women alike, much of it related to the roles played in childhood.

Robert Bly once asked an audience if they realized what it is like as a man not only to see a woman show her feelings but also to reach down inside and pull up words for them. Men's socialization has supported their ignoring and protecting emotions. Little wonder that alcoholism treatment for most men deals so exclusively with feelings.

Many of us mothers turned our boys over to their dads out of our fear of creating "sissies." Family therapist Olga Silverstein says that in doing so, we helped perpetuate the pattern and cheated our boys of receiving training in interpersonal relationship skills. (And we are upset later when our adult male children do not communicate as effectively or as often as we would like!) As a result, many men rely on a crisis to awaken dormant feelings.

Since we are socialized into the art and practice of emotional intimacy, female caretakers of relationships often find it easier to express their feelings. Yet I can also say that expressiveness is not gender-bound. I hear both men and women acknowledge their emotional inadequacy. Too often I see them buying into the messages of pop psychology books that focus mostly on differences. Many such books assert that these characteristics are innate and unchangeable. I do not agree. Through the years as I have watched scores of men going through crises of health, career, or families, I have seen them find expressiveness.

In recent years I have seen a fascinating phenomenon: Some women who have been pleading for years with their male partners for intimacy feel confused and overwhelmed when they finally get what they've been asking for. Many of these women acknowledge that they then send "change back" messages to their male partner. This dynamic is understandable because we have all, men and women alike, accepted the cultural stereotype of what men and women should be.

A client of mine illustrates how these stereotypes can be used to cover fear. Jason, in a successful public relations career, asked me intensely, "But what if something better comes along?" Jason had many superficial relationships. At age thirty-six, he has had what I call "the untilness syndrome" most of his adult years. He's always watching for exits and new beginnings. He never fully steps into the circle of commitment because his consumer attitude keeps him "shopping." He waits; he will not commit. "Until the best job comes along, and the 'right' relationship," he asserts.

He searches frenetically for possible commitments through aborted community involvements, workout programs, travel, and occasional one-night stands. Jason knows little about delayed gratification. Obtaining his college degree was the major commitment in his life. Since then he has seemed committed only to maintaining his man-about-town image.

Probing for the origins of his beliefs, I asked about love relationships. He said, "She's history." Regarding jobs, he replied, "Been there, done that"—another signal that he was skimming the surface of life. He seldom gathered enough history to fear endings.

Jason had a fundamental fear of losing his freedom. He felt that his bank account was the only guarantee of external freedom. I commented, "You seem imprisoned by your freedom." He did admit that his ultimate fear is that of not being committed to anything or anyone.

Recently Jason entered into a men's group. At first he was too arrogant to admit that he could be affected by others. Eventually he learned that he feared people. As he became more honest, he revealed, "I am seeing that if I get too close, I give people the power to hurt my pride. I question whether I can ever be committed in this lifetime, or whether I even have the capacity to commit." This was a major revelation for Jason; he faced his climb and he committed to it. Now he better understands the underlying reasons for his inability to make commitments.

By avoiding risks, a person can avoid serious commitments. This behavior reminds me of the adage that a ship in a port is safe, but that's not what it is built for. For some the fear is not the climb to commitment, but the commitment to climb at all.

Yet you don't have to stay unmarried to avoid intimacy. Rod, a forty-five-year-old poet and naturalist, entered therapy when he ended his fourth marriage by engaging in his fourth "bail-out" affair. He said, in a romanticized tone, "Life is short; we don't know what tomorrow will bring." I stared at him and responded, "I know that you know deep inside that this is just another grand justification so that you can continue your desperate search to fill your loneliness and avoid intimacy. I am asking you not to see this new woman for at least three months." Rod winced sheepishly and said, "I'm being found out—I guess that won't work anymore, will it?" The pressure added by his estranged and disgusted adult children further pushed Rod to examine his behavior.

Some would describe Rod's story as a typical case of male commitment phobia. Protective friends told him, "These changes are part of your growth." He admitted that whenever he felt bored or stuck in a marriage, he would begin an affair with someone who would then soon become his next wife. Rod did not know what it was to commit to a relationship. He decided to examine the roots and logic of his thinking.

Rod admitted that he had been attempting to fill his loneliness with serial relationships. He said he not only feared loneliness but, worse than that, "I'm afraid there is truly nothing inside me." He soon learned that his struggle was not at all about change—it was about going deep. He said, "I have no idea what true intimacy is." In therapy he learned to feel the ache of his loneliness, the signal of his longing for connection.

When Rod brought his two daughters into therapy, he began to feel deep remorse for his deceptive behavior. When one daughter asked painful questions about his secretive behavior, he responded openly and committed to being honest "from now on." Rod, like most of us, wanted to be the most of who he could be for his children.

I assured Rod that many of us make decisions by default—from automatic unconscious patterns. He saw it was not too late to learn. I said, "We're only young once, but we can be immature all of our lives." Rod went deeper into his aloneness and found some solitude. He began to know what and who mattered to him.

Rod ended his current affair so that he could create space for grieving his losses and focus on working to interrupt his self-sabotaging cycle. He said he had heard that men don't grieve; they just replace. Rod deepened his relationships with his daughters. He renewed his commitments—this time from his heart, his caring. He realized his fear of loss and grief was behind his avoidance of any gap between relationships.

While fear is often covered by denial, it can also be totally ignored through manipulative behavior. A client, Gil, a forty-nine-year-old speech teacher, had made his decision to leave his marriage of ten years but was afraid of his wife Celia's anger. Throughout the entire process he talked tentatively to Celia, who constantly misread his messages. She thought he was ambivalent about leaving. Actually, Gil was not ambivalent at all; he was trying to grease his exit ramp. This long, drawn-out process was not only hard on Celia but also on their two boys, who were also very confused because they too misread their dad's messages. Reacting to his unintended dishonesty, Gil's children picked up on the anger felt by their mother, whom they felt sorry for, and they were angry with Gil for almost a year. When Gil sought help, he learned how harmful his strategy had been and sat down with his family to begin taking responsibility for his intentions.

Sometimes, however, avoiding intimacy stems from a fear of engulfment.

Fear of Engulfment

The following case is a reminder of how injuries from childhood have to be faced. George, a thirty-three-year-old electrical engineering student, struggled in his relationship with Sue. He told her he really cared, but he wanted to go slowly. He made certain that he had time to hunt with his men friends, but had difficulty committing even to a Saturday night date with Sue. She made it easy for him; she gave him the power to make most decisions. He seemed to be in control of their relationship, and issues from her past she had not faced, along with her genuine respect for him, kept her in. She thought seriously about not seeing him, but then she heard the story behind his fear of engulfment and decided to be more patient.

George had grown up in a family with two sisters and a mother who had become the sole parent after her husband walked out. Early on, his mother turned to George for emotional closeness, making him male head of household. He had felt responsible for his sisters. In his caretaking he had consistently drowned his own feelings and thoughts in order to accommodate others. Then, in his early adulthood, he had difficulty separating from all the women in his family.

He repeatedly faced his fear of being swallowed
"giving all" and carefully regulated the distance in his re-
tionships. George had difficulty knowing what he wanted.
At the same time he had roots deep enough to enable him to
take risks. I encouraged George to speak with his mother
and sisters about his fear. He invited all of them into two sessions in my office in which he reviewed with his family
what it had been like for him as a son and as a brother. He
then declared his independence and felt truly understood by
his family members.

George was in the process of learning that he could not
really be swallowed up—only crowded! Shortly after his
family sessions, he met a new woman, Alice, and fell in love—
passionately. George decided that by making a commitment
to Alice, he could work through his previous fears—in a trusting, safe, loving relationship.

Fear of Rejection

I think most of us have felt the fear of rejection at some
time in our lives. One does not have to be deeply scarred by
rejections to know it. Many of us feel rejected because we
misread or misinterpret others' behavior. For example, when
only one person can be hired for a particular job, would you
feel rejected for longer than a few minutes if you weren't the
one? What message would you give to yourself?

One person might say, "I guess I could call and see where
I fell short in the interview or ask what the interviewer was
looking for exactly." Another might say, "There it is again.
No one wants me." Some people live with patterns in which
they set themselves up to be dismissed or rejected, unconsciously loyal to an old message they've told themselves.
Naturally, for those who have known deep wounds of
exclusion, the fear is primary, and we can understand why
they would protect themselves. When rejection has involved
betrayal, the scars seem deepest.

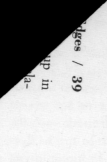

...of mine, Enrico, a copywriter, met Elena, ...who was to become his second wife, he ...s the wedding date approached. He came ...ull-blown anxiety attack after seeing his ...ir prenuptial agreement. His first wife had ...ir marriage abruptly and refused to discuss ...ourt. She had been awarded the home and much of his family money. Deep fears of rejection surfaced in Enrico. "What if Elena leaves me too? I don't know if I can do this; my fear of being rejected is too huge." He said he could not sleep at night, worrying whether he could trust Elena. The fact that the prenuptial agreement was very fair did nothing to assuage his fear. Furthermore, he had no reason to believe that Elena was like his first wife.

I said, "You and Elena have been together for almost two years now. And from all I have seen and heard, you have no present-day reason to fear her rejection." I then repeated a saying a friend has shared often: "If you know you have to swallow a toad, don't look at it too long." Enrico risked; he and Elena have been married seven years.

Fear of Exposure

Fear of exposure can also be caused by shame. This problem as well often has roots deep in childhood. If you grew up in a shame-bound family, you learned exposure was not safe. I am referring to families that keep secret alcoholism, suicides, children born out of wedlock, sexual preferences, and even ethnicity. These systems demand control, perfectionism, blame, and denial. For many of us, revealing ourselves meant eliciting name calling, ridicule, unkind teasing, put-downs, blaming, and verbal assaults. The result is that we often carry unconscious fears that keep us feeling small and insignificant. We hide early shaming and/or abusive experiences that have not been worked through behind a protective inner armor called a false self, which protects us from feeling shamed. And we all learn ways to cover our fear.

Climbing out of conformity is difficult because we climb away from what is comfortable—and risk not being liked. It took me years to realize that my accommodation of others was not always sincere; at times it had a lot to do with my need to be liked. I live in a state with a communication style that many out-of-state people often refer to as "Minnesota nice." We are stereotyped as speaking indirectly and politely. While there is safety in such politeness, and much to be said for it, there is also a bland downside. Minnesota poet Patricia Hampl expressed it clearly, "I come from people who have always been polite enough to feel that nothing has ever happened to them."

Angie seemed not only polite but friendly to everyone she met. If a friend let her down, she would be sad, not angry. Those of us around her would challenge her, trying to elicit her anger. Angie headed a large medical institution, but because she made commitments to many others out of her fear of not being liked, others often swept up after her. Angie often walked away from her true thoughts and feelings to protect or accommodate someone else.

In talking with Angie I learned that she had grown up in a family that literally did not speak to one another. Even dinners were in silence. Her mother sat alone every day playing the piano and never had conversations with anyone except to give minimum directions about chores. Her father did not talk either, unless it was to verbally abuse her brother. Angie grew up with a void of interaction. She had no sense of what she really believed outside her work world, and while she had learned to achieve and become a competent worker, her self-esteem was still low, after all her outward successes.

She had a deep fear of not being liked and finally, through participating in a women's group, learned to stand up for herself. Angie needed to learn to like herself enough to give up the need to be liked by everyone else. Like many women, Angie's identity came from her caring in relationships, and her caring, along with her intelligence, prepared her for her career as a health care administrator.

I can't speak about being liked without returning to gender. Women's socialization has focused on the ethic of care. Yet when we speak our thoughts honestly, we enhance our self-esteem. I think we have all known people who have entered into commitments out of the fear of not being liked, or displeasing someone, and have seen them cheat themselves in the process.

Fear of the Unknown

Commitment has a hold on the future, and the future holds the unknown. Facing the unknown can be terrifying. This is particularly true because we all desire control in our lives. Maybe through technological advances we have grown to believe that we should be able to control relationships just as we control the rest of our lives. To commit is often to take risks, yet eventually we learn that if we stay within ourselves, our individual traits work just fine.

For me, fear of the unknown and fear of giving up control are inseparable. This is where personal history often meets cultural history. My friend Duane put it this way: "When other kids in school took band and soccer, I took control." Duane grew up in a disruptive, volatile family and needed to take control of himself and his decisions to protect himself. In his childhood years he was overwhelmed with chaos and abuse. To suggest to him that he let go would certainly be of no help. Step by step, he learned to lessen his need for control, and as he developed more personal safety, he was able to take risks and live more comfortably with the unknown.

Often I have closed workshops in a circle, offering an

Ojibway prayer that I refer to as a three-step prayer: "I step into the day; I step into myself; I step into the mystery." When we surrender to the unknown, awe and fear often join hands. While the unknown can certainly hold suffering, it also holds opportunities.

Through risking, adventure can become an "inventure" as well. My friend Dick Leider coined the phrase *inventure* to describe the inner journey of creating challenges to propel our self-discovery and growth. As I learned to trust the unknown, I became aware of the aliveness I felt.

Time and time again my teacher, the wilderness, has taught me that I can engage in challenges while filled with fear. The mind does hold "mountains." A sense of adventure captured me. It seemed that my commitment to outdoor adventures was closely tied to self-discovery. I often found that on the other side of the fear lay growth, awareness, and confidence.

I saw how fear blocks the good feelings we get from endorphins, the opium-like neurotransmitters in our brain. Have you ever felt a "runner's high"? We know that even positive thoughts can raise endorphin levels and alleviate chronic pain. Have you ever asked yourself why human beings choose to put themselves at risk? I think we take risks—from low-level to frightening, life-threatening experiences—to push our "growing" edges and integrate more of ourselves. Fear is functional in that way. Fear can excite that essential edge that keeps our commitments alive.

Grammy Award–winning vocalist and jazz improvisor Bobby McFerrin, creative director of the St. Paul Chamber Orchestra, said in 1989 that at one point he was on autopilot, trapped in himself. He told about walking out on a concert stage and feeling absolutely no fear. Although still committed to his life of music, he knew he needed a new "edge," a new mountain of the mind. He consequently made several changes in his performance life that eventually led him to become even more versatile. He began to study conducting.

Even though McFerrin had been highly acclaimed with fame and honors, he knew we do not learn on top of the mountain. We learn through the climbing, through the experience. McFerrin was courageous. His climb meant facing new fears, and more than that, he acted in response to his own true being. I believe the McFerrin story struck me because he stated so clearly how important it is to have the edge of fear to ignite our growth. By facing our fears we can become more of who we are, a more authentic self.

I recall a story from my own experience in learning how to accept the unknown. Fear was awakened in me when I booked a room at a Kathmandu hotel that my New Delhi Indian guide had strongly recommended. When I saw no mention of Dwarika House in my travel guides, I feared for my health. Would the water be safe? Amebic dysentery is so prevalent in the Himalayas. Would I have been better off at the Holiday Inn? Had I taken the guide's suggestion just to be polite? Just what had I gotten into? I felt anxious.

Upon my arrival at Dwarika House, I heaved a sigh of relief and smiled to myself, realizing that my fear was groundless. The place was unique, a charming guest house built of old brick and ancient woods, filled with Hindu and Buddhist art, in a setting of beautifully planted grounds. And yes, they had purified water. The Dwarikas were warm, welcoming people and invited me to a fireside dinner that night with other foreign guests.

My stay at the Dwarika House was a supportive start for my trek. I felt a spirit in both place and people in Nepal. My fears of an unknown land fell away quickly. I warmed to the friendly, constant greeting, spoken with bowed head and prayer-filled hands—"Namaste," meaning, "I honor the divine within you."

All the stories here show how our fear-based beliefs reside deep within us. Fear affects all the other inner climbs.

We do not stop losing power by refusing to recognize our fear, by numbing ourselves to what we feel. By facing our fears we can move slowly ahead on our path to an authentic, committed life.

Chapter 3

Trust: The Covenant

"Trust. Create. Be who you are. The rest is up to your nonphysical Teachers and the Universe." —Gary Zukav

MT. MERU, TANZANIA, EAST AFRICA. *Burning candles cast a soft glow on the boarded-up windows of a hut constructed of crude planks. I learned that these planks had been hand-carried to the 11,000-foot saddle of Mt. Meru. Awaiting our ascent, we were filled with excitement and unspoken tension. Mt. Meru, with its crested peaks, looked like a giant dinosaur lying fully stretched out across the African plain. Its base was so long, it hardly looked its 15,500 feet.*

Today was a full hiking day. Our spirits had sagged by the time we arrived at the hut tonight. The hearty stew and pasta dinner was just what we needed for the climb only seven hours away. We ate quickly and carefully sorted our gear while there was still some light. Now only the sounds of whispered conversations are audible; we all want to be rested for our two a.m. rising. We all share a secret; we are tense with fear and mistrust. We don't talk about it until the next day.

We left the hut around two o'clock this morning in pitch dark, our way lighted by a sliver of moonlight and powerful flashlights. We carried little in our packs. Naturalist-guide Thad, of Dorobo Safaris, my co-leader and friend, often referred to as a "white

Maasai," carried some small branches and a teapot in his pack for tea at the top.

The start was steep; we struggled as we planted our walking sticks and slogged through tall grasses soaked with early morning dew. Those in the group who had expected to face hard rock at the outset were greatly disappointed. "After all, it is a mountain!" they groaned. At times, occasional steep slopes of smooth, slick mud demanded that we make vertical lunges. Each move required concentration and balance. We planted each foot carefully, knowing it would take even more energy if we fell and had to right ourselves. One of the guides and I sang for a while, but few others joined in; it took too much effort and seemed contrived. Actually, it was contrived; I was attempting to inject some energy and gently nudge some members of the group out of the fears that I could see were absorbing them. I learned later the singing had irritated a few of them. They obviously knew better than I had that they needed to preserve their energy.

Two of the twelve climbers turned back within the first hour, feeling discouraged and distrustful of their physical abilities. Thankfully, Thad and I had decided to bring extra porters should this happen. Still, doubt crept into me: Was this a mistake? This was the trip of a lifetime for many in the group who anticipated exciting, esteem-building experiences. They had not signed on for wilderness therapy. Did I trust myself? Would the group trust our decision to make this climb? Could I trust that Thad would remember trails that he had not taken since his high school days?

As the trails improved, so did our spirits. Finally, we reached a true winding trail, albeit only about eight inches wide, but an identifiable trail nonetheless. At 13,000 feet, we saw fresh elephant droppings! No one appeared frightened by this surprise. Perhaps we were focused so intensely on hiking that we blocked our fear, or perhaps we were at the point in our safari where we felt accustomed to such surprises. I was concerned. "What other animals might be here?" I asked myself. "Can I trust that this mountain is not too dangerous?"

Within the hour, two more climbers turned back, mistrusting

their ability to reach the summit. I began to worry anew; a knot grew in my stomach. We had not brought along that many extra porters to take them down! Yet I did not want to raise anxieties by saying, "If you think you're going to turn back, do it now!" Usually, I "reconnaissance" a climb to determine its appropriateness for inexperienced climbers. This time I had put all my trust in Thad. Besides, we had just completed a two-week walking safari, so we were in good condition. Still, my self-doubt mushroomed. Focusing on my breathing, I decided I had to trust—the only choice.

It was still dark when we reached some rock outcroppings, which gave us solid footing. Then we flashed our beams on what appeared to be an ancient reptilian-like rock form rising before us. We had no choice but to walk its spiny back. The guides called this "creature" Rhinoceros Back because of the pile of rhinoceros bones that mysteriously lies at its highest point. There is a sheer drop from either side of the top "spine." I felt grateful for the darkness; I couldn't know what lay ahead. Still, anxiety about our safety jangled inside me.

Discouraged and angry, three more climbers turned back. After a thorough discussion in which Thad and I expressed our respect for their choices and reined in our natural urge to persuade, we said our good-byes. I had to remind myself that this trek was "inward bound," not a survival course. What a vivid example this was of the betrayal we experience when reality fails to match our expectations!

We went on, gingerly making our way across the spiny ridge. "Pole, pole" (pronounced "polee, polee") was our mantra— "slowly, slowly" in Swahili. I talked to my feet, I talked with the Goddess or God or whoever would listen, and I continued to focus on my breathing. Slowly, slowly; trusting, trusting. My trust was not betrayed; as we began our descent to broader rock expanses, my anxiety lessened with each step.

This challenge seemed to be in preparation for the rest of the climb during which we would face some fearful trails and turns. The sky was stingy with light that morning, as though a decision had been made to have a slow-motion day. A dark watercolor background wash subdued the morning light. We longed for a sudden burst of bright sunlight. Very gradually the dawn came and shone in encouragement on us.

Mt. Meru is deceptive. When I saw the peak straight ahead, I commented excitedly, "That's it!" Augustino, one of our African guides, pointed toward the peak ahead and said, "Yes, Ma'lyn," in that familiar Swahili way that sounded more like "melon." With our hearts beating faster, we quickened our pace with the bursting, wriggling energy of schoolchildren told to walk safely and slowly during a fire drill. Soon, however, we discovered that what we had spotted was not the peak of Mt. Meru but rather another one of those crested dinosaur peaks we had seen from below! Augustino had not been trying to deceive me; I think it was the combination of language differences, high winds, and my selective interpretation.

Feelings flooded me: anger first, then disappointment, and then an eruption of willfulness to continue. Once more I learned that the challenge of a climb cannot be measured by the height of the mountain. We steadily made our way upward, peak after peak, resting along the way as needed. Our spirits rose and fell almost rhythmically with each "false" peak. Three of the group went on ahead with Thad. I told him I would "sweep"—that is, remain at the back of the group. Since I did not want to face disappointment again, I no longer asked, "Is that the true top?"

After surmounting several seductive false peaks, we finally saw a small flag marking the summit of Mt. Meru. A surge of energy hastened our climb. Clumsily making our way over giant boulders, we felt simultaneously ebullient and exhausted. I was aware of how little room there was at the top. As Thad's group welcomed us with hugs, we all participated in a traditional Native American ritual of burning sage and sweetgrass.

We felt the combined exhilaration and group spirit of having shared the climb. Some hot tea gave us a final burst of renewed spirit. I observed the group quickly to see how everyone felt. Everyone showed determination, high spirits, and a willingness to trust. Low, dark clouds reminded us that we could not linger. With elation and deep satisfaction, we gathered our gear.

We no sooner had started our descent when the mountain

seemed to say, "Don't get too cocky now; here's a little hail to con-tinue your test." Even so, the descent was surprisingly comfortable; we moved quite nimbly down the rocks, playfully sliding in scree, letting our excitement carry us. When we finally reached the hut, we met the other porters, who reported that the climbers who had turned back had returned safely to the lodge below. We were just at the right level of weariness when we finally joined the rest of the group. I was secretly grateful that we no longer felt the enthusiasm and endorphin rush that had come from the climb. That exhilaration would have been a painful reminder to the others about what they had missed. Our energy seemed tamed and warm enough to join with them without any hidden withholding of excitement.

I was relieved to be down. I thought we should rename Mt. Meru "Mt. Trust," for that is what had drawn us out of our fear, often just a step at a time. As we were coming down the mountain, I had wondered, "How do you commit if you don't trust?" On Mt. Meru, fears had mixed with trust, and as often happens, fear precipitated the final decision. It was the lack of trust in themselves, not their lack of physical ability, that had prompted some climbers to retreat.

On Mt. Meru, I learned viscerally the connection be-tween trust and commitment. Trust is primary to any rela-tionship; it is the covenant in commitment. I use the word covenant because of the sense of solemnity generated by our putting total reliance—some would call it faith—in the space between ourselves and others.

Climbing Mt. Meru forced me to ask, "Just what is trust?" For years I have defined trust as the reliance upon the nonverbal communication of another person to achieve a desired but uncertain goal in a risky situation. How easy it is to say, "I trust you," yet words can deceive. When choosing someone to belay me on my climbs, I make this decision intuitively, from my inner sense of knowing, not on the basis of a person's words or muscles. When we are in a risky situation, little is hidden in our body communication. Stanford University studies have shown that our nonverbal communication is five times more believable than our words. Often we read this nonverbal behavior with our intuition.

Trusting Your Intuition

During a business consultation a man asked "How can I know if my mistrust is truly my solid gut knowing or is something from my past?" I told him that was an excellent question, one that we all face. Pointing at his stomach, he continued, "Do you mean to tell me that there is something in here that actually will tell me whether to trust or not?" Several people responded by nodding their heads.

Often, the key lies in the degree of intensity around the relationship. If you feel highly intense in your mistrust, then you might well have projected some unresolved family-of-origin ghost, or some past event, onto the scene. In the past I often asked myself, "Does this person or situation remind me of anyone close to me, or any incident, from my past? How intensely do I feel about this person?"

We then discussed how each of us could remember times when we trusted and were bruised. We also discussed how often we ignored a flash of mistrust. Most of us can look back and realize that it is through our learning experiences over the years that we learn whom we can trust. Now I realize how good I had been at "apparently trusting"— which at the time I thought was real trust. Gradually I learned to trust my mistrust. Our deepening intuition can guide us if we pay attention to it.

We all have had moments when our intuition was not acute enough and we felt our trust ragged. These experiences have taught us to develop our personal wisdom. As we learn to deepen our own self-knowing and self-trust, we are more fully able to live with the dialectical tension of knowing that being an adult is learning to live with paradox and ambiguity.

Under stress, gender difficulties often reveal themselves. In my work on my doctoral dissertation, I used rock climbing to examine couples' relationships enrichment. I gave a questionnaire on trust to each of the men and women on two different climbing trips. I wanted to validate, using rating scales, my observations about climbing's powerful impact on trust as well as self-esteem, coping with stress, and intimacy.

My findings showed that when men and women ranked trust—in themselves, in the equipment, and in their partner—women trusted their partner most, the equipment second, and themselves least. The opposite held true for men, who trusted themselves first, the equipment second, and their partner third. I had never thought about trust and gender until I saw these results. At first I was surprised to see how low the women had rated themselves on the self-trust scale. And then I said, "Of course!" These results clearly amplified what most women and men already know— women are not socialized to trust themselves physically. Yet when the women had completed a four-day rock-climbing course, a six-week follow-up questionnaire revealed that their self-trust scores *tripled* those of the men's—a dramatic increase. And to top it all off, everyone's self-esteem was considerably higher than it had been before the climbing trip.

I was excited to see the dramatic shift evoked by climbing. During fireside discussions the women said how much stronger they felt—not physically but in inner strength. They felt an added confidence in themselves. In contrast, the men talked about what it was like to face their feelings and their vulnerability. Women and men realized that when climbing, their internalized learning about gender was indelibly clear. They talked through the late hours about how they had not acknowledged their lack of self-trust and how that had affected their relationships.

This was shown vividly by one couple. Chang and Mei Lee, both thirty-seven years old, had been in group psycho-therapy for over a year as a required part of their medical school training. During one of our first North Shore rock-climbing trips for psychiatry residents, they faced a major threat to their two-year engagement and wedding plans. The incident began when Chang was to be the support person, the belayer, for Mei Lee, who was preparing to rappel down the cliff. As she stood facing him, she had only to step back and lower herself over the edge and down the cliff. Mei Lee froze. The assembled group of climbers were there to reas-sure her. "You can do it. You're all set to go now." Chang smiled patiently, saying, "Remember, it's me here; I've got you!"

Suddenly, the calm and steady Mei Lee exploded in anger and screamed, "No way, I don't trust you! You can't belay me! I don't trust you! I won't marry you!" Tears followed as she untied from her belay and climbing ropes with trembling, fumbling fingers. Mei Lee seemed as surprised as the rest of us at her outburst. Embarrassed, the couple stood embracing and then sat together under a tree to talk. They were shocked that after a year of psychotherapy together there were any issues of trust to be addressed. She later said that she had no idea where the explosion had come from. I recalled an old Shaker adage: "Don't try to reason someone out of something they didn't reason into." She graphically learned how powerful a hold the unconscious has on the body. Mei Lee also learned that a great deal of her mistrust had nothing to do with Chang. She had very little trust in herself, since she had badly misplaced trust in two prior long-term relationships in which she had felt betrayed.

As Mei Lee discovered, trust lies at the foundation of relationships. A climber's rope symbolizes the connection of commitment between people. Our trust gets frayed at times.

Through our relationships we learn what climbing mountains teaches—the need to trust ourselves in order to trust others. In this case, Mei Lee and Chang decided to postpone their wedding for a year to work on trust.

Basis of Trust

It takes a long time to learn to trust our gut feelings. We can all recall moments when a flash of intuition warned us—don't trust—and we ignored it, to our regret. Many who learned early in life that expression of feelings was not safe, or acceptable, protected themselves through a shutdown of feelings, or emotional amnesia. This lack of awareness about feelings is a true disability. I have often wondered if we marked parking spaces for the "emotionally disabled" as we do for the physically disabled, how crowded our parking lots would be.

Our basic sense of trust is established in our early lives through the constancy of the child-caregiver relationship. I have often seen adults who have lied to themselves about their low level of trust that began in childhood. Children often bury their mistrust and blanket it with denial. Sometimes this denial is born out of a need to protect an old family secret. "There's nothing going on here—and don't tell anybody" is often the implicit rule in families who keep secrets about mental illness, affairs, alcoholism, or suicide attempts. I have found that as I discharge the negative energy covering old, buried feelings of hurt or fear, I deepen my trust in others. I can then expand my capacity to connect with others.

Jack, a fifty-eight-year-old airline executive, had learned to be an engaging personality. Known as a good listener, he and his partner, Jose, a furniture designer, were popular dinner guests. One evening at a dinner party, he spent almost the entire dinner drawing out the woman seated next to him and learned much about her. When dessert came, the woman turned to Jack with a big smile. "You know, I want to tell you I know something. I too fear being exposed, and I truly know what you are up to with all this focus on me because I typically do the same thing myself." Jack sputtered, pulled his chair back a bit, readjusted himself, and then burst out laughing at being discovered. "You are dead right," he exclaimed. He then added, "But I usually get away with it."

Without defending himself, he was able to acknowledge his scar tissue from the shameful exposure of his past, when he was mocked and mimicked in his emotionally abusive family. They agreed they had both come upon a creative coping strategy to cover their fear of exposure.

Despite the importance of childhood security to trust, it is not the only factor. Life experiences shape our trust as well. Serious harm can cause trust to shut down at any age, like this experience of a fellow traveler shows.

Maggie, a computer analyst, and Shirley, a high-energy banker, were rooming together in Guilin Guest State House after a Li River boat tour and biking tour to an archeological dig. We were all quite tired that evening when we went off to our rooms, which were clustered together on the third floor of the hotel. Maggie, age thirty-six, and Shirley, age sixty-two, were undressing for bed about midnight when they heard a knock at their door. Alert and frightened, they decided not to respond. The person went away. Within five minutes their telephone rang, and when they answered, all they could discern was some garbled English and some "heavy breathing." Her anxieties rising, Maggie quickly hung up, certain that someone must be stalking them. She thought she had heard him say, "I want you . . ." "I think he wants something, and it felt sexual," Maggie said in a high, tightly choked voice.

After a second call from the man with the same breathy voice, Shirley told Maggie, "We'd better get out of here." A duet of panic began. Maggie replied, "But how? We already know there has been someone in the hall; that won't be safe!" Highly anxious, Shirley said, "I've got the perfect plan. Jock and Mike are rooming together right around the corner. In fact, we can see their windows from here. If we raise our windows and walk the ledge, then we can go into their room for protection."

Maggie agreed, and they began to traverse the third-floor window ledge, hugging the wall and windows and slowly making their way to Jock and Mike's room.

Jock and Mike were shocked when they heard the tapping at the windows but quickly opened them fully so that the women could enter. While Shirley was climbing through the window, she wrenched her ankle. After relating their night of terror, she lay down with her foot elevated.

Early the next morning, I heard a loud knocking at my door and opened it to a highly excited Maggie and Shirley, who poured forth their story tearfully and angrily. I was indignant yet deeply troubled by their dramatic actions. "How can this be? Can't our women feel safe in this guest house?" We marched downstairs to the front desk and demanded to see the manager. When he arrived, I proclaimed, "Our women are not safe here. Someone tried to enter their room last night." Again, Maggie and Shirley poured their story forth, this time struggling to speak slowly so that they could be understood. The manager listened intently, and periodically I inserted, "Our women must feel safe here." The manager said he would check with his night staff.

The manager returned shortly, stating that perhaps he could help. He said, "Someone on duty indeed called the room." He then attempted to reassure us that his staff were not trying to harass the women, at which point I suspiciously interrupted, "Just where is this person who worked the night shift?" The manager quickly produced the "culprit"—a slight seventeen-year-old youth who had been attempting, first by knocking on the door and then by telephoning, to ask the two women to shut their windows since the air conditioning was on. The women stared in shock as they heard him explain.

As we talked in the car en route to the hospital to have Shirley's broken ankle set in a cast, Maggie told a story of being sexually assaulted ten years earlier. The telephone calls the night before had rekindled her memory and flooded her with fear and mistrust, which she had projected onto the hotel staff and the entire incident. Every sound, every word fed her fear. She had struggled for years to know whom to trust.

Injuries to trust can have far-reaching consequences if they aren't confronted and then resolved. Our entire view of the world can be jaundiced, making any meaningful commitment impossible. For one of my clients, her future was at stake because she couldn't face up to an injury in her past.

Anita, a finance specialist, had reached the highest level ever achieved by a woman in her corporation. In an almost desperate tone she told me that the company's president had challenged her about her supposed commitment to the company. Anita told me that she didn't make commitments so she wouldn't be hurt. When I asked her where that thinking came from, she said that she had made that decision almost twenty years earlier, when her mother had been deemed terminally ill. Anita had made a commitment to God: "If you heal my mother and let her live, I'll live a good, honest, clean life." Miraculously, her mother had lived.

Deeply struck by the impact of her commitment to God and goodness, Anita was thrilled. For the first six months she led an exemplary life as she had promised. As time went on, however, she broke her pledge by using drugs and engaging in promiscuous sexual behavior with married men she met in bars. She plunged into self-destructive relationships.

During the peak of Anita's acting-out period, her mother died. Anita felt that she had betrayed her mother and her God and was solely responsible for her mother's death. She made a shame-filled vow to herself that since she could not be trusted to make any commitment of any kind, she would make none. Anita had never disclosed her vow to anyone and had worked hard to reinvent herself. She had been quite successful so far, but now her job was at stake. She had to do something about her commitment.

Obviously, Anita had to accept that she did not have the power to kill her mother—or keep her alive. She also learned that the covenant she had broken was the covenant with herself about how she wanted to conduct her life. She saw it was a setup to fail. Anita had not trusted herself enough to commit again. She truly thought that since she had broken her "deal" with God, she was facing natural punitive consequences.

Anita's thinking took a major turn as she grieved the loss of her mother in a genuine, unpunishing way. She then moved on to making commitments at work and in her social world, beginning the step-by-step pathway to building trust in her relationships. Anita's president commented on her changes and gave her a higher position with responsibility in executive leadership training.

Sometimes trust issues do not surface because people place their trust in an institution, such as marriage, rather than each other. I recall a dramatic awakening to this awareness when a client had a traumatic injury.

Blind Trust

David, a star professional athlete, married Janice because he decided "it was time to marry" and he was tired of his "different woman in every city" pattern. Janice, about six years younger than David, was impressed to be dating this popular "image" and thought of him as a wonderful catch. They cemented their relationship in its early stages with drugs and sex. Both came from strong Italian Philadelphia families who supported their marriage. David left athletics so that he could be home more. Janice's maternal grandfather took David into the family's successful wholesale grocery business. Within a year Janice was pregnant. By external measures, it was a good start.

As both became invested in their traditional roles, their drug use diminished. David became psychologically absent as he dived into his new job, and Janice seldom complained. She filled her life with family and friends. As the children approached their school years, Janice, more aware of David's lack of family involvement, grew increasingly irritated and sarcastic. David retreated, which escalated the tension. The pattern seemed set; she intruded and he retreated. Feeling despondent, David asked Janice to go with him to see a therapist. She refused, saying that he had only to be more present when he was home and everything would be all right.

Then a trauma interrupted their fixed pattern. David was hospitalized for a spinal cord injury incurred during a high dive. Not knowing what the outcome could be, he felt terror for the first time in his life. The accident proved to be his "wake up call"—for the first time in his adult life he was vulnerable, and his lens of perception dramatically shifted.

When Janice arrived late at the hospital, she seemed to lack sympathy. David's long-denied feelings of mistrust suddenly surfaced and engulfed him like a tidal wave. He was hurt and confused. During the long hours in his hospital bed, he reviewed his life and began to face his "gut knowing"— hearing his own voice. He said, "I see I've been living a lie. I have been lonely almost all of my life, and now know I am in an empty marriage." He realized that he had lied to himself about their being there for each other. He said the mutual disrespect and sarcasm were too painful; he had to make changes.

When David left the hospital, grateful that he could function quite well, he again asked Janice to enter therapy with him. Again she refused. David said that he would leave if she did not come with him, so she reluctantly attended two sessions. She said that he just had to change and everything would be all right. David continued in therapy alone.

He examined his own emotional dishonesty. He discovered he had never been committed to himself—or to Janice. He said he didn't know who he was or who she was. Their commitment had been to the institution of marriage rather than to their relationship. Janice had been doing what the culture had taught her—living a role as a good wife and mother. In addition, she had never truly left her own family emotionally.

Divorce was frowned on by David's Catholic family; he did not want to divorce, so he became more involved with the family for more than a year. As a result, he felt much closer to his children, but he still felt the emptiness in his marriage.

David finally spoke to Janice of a separation; she pleaded with him to stay, suddenly relinquishing all her power to him. She said she would do anything it took—except professional help. David struggled with his dilemma. He began to talk openly and honestly about his feelings for the first time. When he pushed to change their marriage, it began to crumble rapidly. He could not trust the new Janice, and Janice did not trust herself enough to take a stand about her own needs.

In time, David chose divorce. Through the mediation process he vividly learned that a bad marriage can be more hurtful to children than a divorce. Ironically, as is often the case, when one partner chooses healthy growth, it fractures the fixed patterns that holds the marriage together. David and Janice soon realized their love for their children was far stronger than their disappointment and anger with each other.

It takes many of us a long time to trust ourselves intellectually and stand up for what we think. We need a secure base of knowledge and the courage to speak credibly. Mark

Suwyn, CEO and board chair of Louisiana Pacific, is a prime example of a person who trusts himself.

For the past decade he has been committed to changing the corporate culture to create a work environment of respect and cooperation. His vision includes letting people know they matter and that they make a difference. Mark did not have this philosophy in his younger days, yet today he is comfortable with people at all levels—from the workers in the plants to his colleagues in the boardroom. Clearly, this is not the outcome of his traditional corporate training. Mark's story is extraordinary in that it exemplifies the trust that comes from stirring intuitive knowing into rational thinking while leading an entire organization in reshaping the work environment.

Mark had started working almost full-time in the seventh grade. He had put himself through college and earned his Ph.D. in chemistry while supporting a student-wife and a young child. As the years passed, he gained a real appreciation of work of all kinds and a deep sense of justice and its place in the workplace. After college, Mark moved up rapidly in the business world. He was a senior vice-president at DuPont when an incident occurred that would become the catalyst for his vision. Mark had a moment of "gut knowing" in a meeting during which senior management rationalized why two accomplished senior executive women resigned for what Mark knew were unclear reasons. As head of human resources, he sought them out and learned: "It was just too hard to exist in the hostile working environment at DuPont." Mark said he began to realize he was working in an exclusionary management environment that hired for sameness, an environment made up almost entirely of "people just like me." Mark knew intuitively that he had to be educated about diversity and brought in two outside consultants to work with a racially mixed core group of men and women to become more respectful of diversity within DuPont.

Mark recognized that people cannot survive in a system where some might feel emotionally brutalized by the verbal abuse of those in positions of power. He said he hadn't realized that he implicitly accepted what he refers to as his "white, male, comfortable, positive style of power and privilege."

Mark had a vision of thousands of people with a new consciousness of a vital, diversified, friendly environment. This led to hundreds of employees participating in week-long multicultural workshops and many changes in policies and practices.

During same time period Mark met Magaly Rodriguez, an energetic, sensitive business consultant whose philosophy and technologies fit with Mark's vision. He asked her to come into DuPont to work toward changing its culture. Mark realized that his tools to support his philosophy had to be integrated throughout his organization. As his commitment to change deepened, he realized he was stepping off the path to becoming CEO at DuPont. He left DuPont to join International Paper.

In his new position, Mark solidified his commitment by taking his entire sector through Rapid Change Technologies, a program developed by Magaly and Carol Cappuzzo and Karen Lundquist, her two colleagues at Creative Breakthroughs, Inc. There they instituted a Breakthrough Leadership Program in which they focused on teaching what Daniel Goleman refers to as "emotional intelligence," which involves integrating empathy, intuition, respect, and caring as the route to significant growth and improvement. Mark personally attended scores of the training sessions to continue deepening his understanding and to support the learning of others.

There were serious problems to be addressed: a downsized workforce, environmental issues, and a chemical-spill lawsuit, to name a few. He took the courageous step of spending time and money to rethink his organizations within the company and to rejuvenate his people. At first employees hesitated to trust that they could speak up honestly. Participants in these sessions learned a communication model that allowed them to deal respectfully with differences and ask for changes. As Mark's lead team members began to learn how to use the technology skills and support each other, they knew they could succeed. He demonstrated that when fairness and respectful communication reign, self-esteem improves. The energy, creativity, and innovation of the organization increased markedly. As a result, the bottom line improved.

All of Mark's actions have purpose. They have run counter to his old learning about manhood, corporations, and power.

Today, at Louisiana Pacific, Mark remains true to his commitment, leading from the heart while watching the bottom line. Once again employees have dared to have hope and to follow his inspirational leadership.

Mark Suwyn is a living model of remarkable intellectual self-trust and commitment to a process. He truly is a long-distance runner; he trusts in a process—committing to his vision to change a culture creatively and gain lasting systemic change. Perhaps what is most powerful about his vision is his personal involvement in the process of change. He attends employee training seminars and listens to his employees either in person or on a speaker telephone. They see that the process of change has taken place from the top down.

Mark's actions are significant since we are living in a time when more than eighty percent of workers from a variety of companies say loyalty has declined in the last seven years. He reminds me of how many of us live without knowing our purpose in life. Mark's own passion is magnetic, and his trust in his ideas and beliefs are truly spearheading an evolution in the dramatically changing world of work.

Not all challenges to trust are personal issues. The effects of family, national, and global events can run the gamut of challenging us physically, emotionally, and intellectually. Through the years my trust has ripened. I am more fully trusting of myself and my values. Faust said that when we trust ourselves, we will know how to live. Our climb of Mt. Meru gave us vivid lessons in trust. Yet there was another factor working along with trust that helped us get to the top—support!

Chapter 4

Support: Life Anchors

"Those whom we support hold us up in life."
—Marie von Ebner-Eschenbach

MT. KILIMANJARO, TANZANIA, EAST AFRICA. *Kibo Hut, 15,500 feet. It is such a relief to be back down at this hut! As we descended this morning, I felt warmed when I saw our guide, Mr. Remy, bringing us cold, refreshing tea. Mr. Remy's formality is limited to his name; he is actually warm and attentive. A member of the Bantu tribe, known as the "businessman's tribe," that lives at the base of Mt. Kilimanjaro, he takes his work seriously. We had been hiking for eleven hours and had just descended from Gilman's Peak, the 19,360-foot summit of Mt. Kilimanjaro. Our guides gave us permission to rest, but time is rationed here—we are allowed one and a half hours. While this is logical since the air is so thin, our bodies are shouting that we need a half day! So much has happened during the past twenty hours!*

Yesterday we arrived at Kibo exhausted and weary of the wet and cold. By our fifth day on the mountain, we had hiked up through five ecosystems—from forests and tropical plants at the base to volcanic scree at the top. We went to bed at 6:00 p.m. but of course could not sleep; we had that "wired and tired" feeling. Other climbers entering the hut at staggered hours interrupted our anxious attempts to sleep. The sounds of varied accents and languages formed a quilt of multicolored sounds, reminding us that many of the world's cultures come together here.

When Mr. Remy came for us at 1:00 a.m., we were ready to push on. We stepped outside into the clarity of the bountiful night sky, filled with friendly, sparkling stars. I was overwhelmed. We saw a few groups of hikers striding off in a determined gait, charging the mountain, stabbing their ski poles as though each thrust would fix them tightly to the mountainside. Our group totaled nine with porters. We had ski poles and were grateful for their support. We were pleased with Mr. Remy's giant lantern and were comforted by our individual flashlights. We were fortunate—no headaches or altitude sickness so far. We realized it's a matter of luck, and we were appreciative. We were pleased that we had spent an extra day to acclimatize at the second hut, Horombo Hut, at 12,000 feet. The mountain had taught us well; we had learned how to pace ourselves and walk "pole pole." Our moods seemed to want to shift with the weather, yet we each worked at keeping a positive attitude. We relied on "self-talk"—reciting mantras or inspirational "I can do it" phrases as we hiked.

After an hour out we saw silhouetted figures descending, one doubled over and another being carried by two companions. As they came closer, we saw that they were the same "chargers" who had set out when we did. We exchanged glances and continued slowly. There was no room for arrogance here.

A few hours later, we saw dimly sparkling lights. Could it be that we were doing that well? Was it really the top we saw in the distance? We heard Mr. Remy's voice trailing, "Halfway." We wanted to quicken our pace but knew better. We hiked in silence, conserving our energy. Soon the lights became brighter, as did our spirits. We were excited—to think we could do this most difficult night of all so easily! When we approached the lights, we saw that what had appeared to be the halfway spot was really halfway to the halfway site! The lights came from people holding flashlights in the rock "cave" known as Hans Meyer Cave, named after the first European to reach the summit, in 1899. We were disappointed and yet were relieved to have shelter.

After a short rest, we plodded on steadily, discouraged but committed. At one point, solid-bodied, forty-eight-year-old Midge stopped abruptly. "I think we should have a meeting; I think we have gone far enough on this mountain." Midge, a sturdy hiker, was weary. We had talked earlier about how each of us faced a different edge—Midge's "edge" was asking for help. We circled around her and rested with her, gently reminding her of our commitment to the climb. Midge nodded with a faint half smile, indicating she could resume climbing.

At that point Mr. Remy held his ski pole across his back, creating a horizontal handhold for Midge. She accepted his support and took hold firmly. We slowly continued on in silence; talking takes energy.

Some hours later, I felt Mr. Remy's gloved hand on my shoulder, slowly turning me around, away from the mountain. There before me was the most glorious sunrise one could hope for, the sun seeming intentionally to rise slowly enough to give us all the time we needed to take in its full beauty. I found myself bowing to the sun in gratitude spirit—our moving in a group and stopping to rest together had inspired and sustained us to continue climbing. One of the men asked us if we had "taken something." We grinned widely as we told them, "We truly did—we took one another!"

Climbing Mt. Kilimanjaro is not just a physical challenge; it is a test of commitment. I was pleased that this five-day challenge had gone so well. I was grateful that we had done all the long hikes we had throughout the entire three-week trek. The step-by-step pacing gave me time to reflect.

I knew that Midge's experience could well have been my own a few years earlier. The lesson on Mt. Kilimanjaro—support—had been a major life climb for me. I think I have always known how to support others; I was a good belayer. Yet it has taken me years to learn how to ask for support. My life today is much richer knowing this. The lesson is simple: You do it yourself, but you don't do it alone.

Asking for help in my family was almost unknown. At

the time of my divorce many years ago, I sought group therapy. Evidently I knew how to appear so competent that no one would ever think I would need to ask for help with much of anything. My cover was so good that when I arrived at the therapy office, the office manager exclaimed, "Not you, Marilyn! You don't need a group! You don't need therapy!" "Please hear me," I persisted. "I do need a group." She arranged an interview with the group therapist.

The first question the therapist asked me was, "How do you ask for help?" I stared long and hard at her; no words came. She repeated, "How do you ask for help?" Again I stared and finally said quietly, "I don't think I can answer that." This was a starting point. Through therapy I learned not only that I did not know how to ask for help, but also that this issue went deeper. The rule of my family was that no Mason children were to have needs.

I am not alone in needing to learn to ask for help. Like many women and men who believe their own myths of being strong, I think I convinced others that I did not need help. When I listen to my toddler granddaughter, Morgan Elizabeth, ask freely, "Can you help me with this?" I take note and sigh with relief. We have finally broken the rule. As with all our inner climbs, my stories of asking for support read more like a volume in my life than a chapter. It has been a hard, long climb. This was the most difficult of all chapters for me to write because I have had to admit that now I need support.

I'll never forget the time when I was leading a back-packing trip in the Baja just six weeks after abdominal surgery. Carrying a forty-pound pack, I was feeling the stress on my surgically weakened body. My colleague Annie came up and said, "I'm taking some of the weight from your pack; it's too much!" I burst into tears at her supportive act of kindness. As we talked about my tears, I realized that, true to my upbringing, I had not considered asking for help.

Annie knew what I needed. I had not even known that I

needed help. I later painfully saw that I was being loyal to my family rule: Masons do not ask for help. This sounds weird as I state it here, but I lived by the rule so long, it refreshes me to write about it. I had not realized that my toughing it out alone was hard on me or that I was denying Annie the opportunity to be a friend.

Of course, I did know how to ask for support with household chores and family responsibilities. I did poorly at asking for support for my emotional needs—empathy and understanding—from men as well as women. As a result, others were cheated of a chance to help me.

I have felt that at times my clients were a step ahead of me, tweaking me about my own life. My mentor had always said, "If you're not in this for your own growth, get out." I now appreciate the support I have received through the years. I think I often took support for granted and was not very aware about who was in my world. Now I am clear about what relationships I carry in my heart. Support is about "being there" and making ourselves available. My friend Dick suggests we ask people to serve on our own personal "board of directors"—friends who will give guidance and support. Some prefer to think of these people as a "coaching staff."

Gender Differences and Support

Some years ago a colleague and I led a backpack trip into Pariah Canyon, a rock-world wonder that branches off the Colorado River. We had taken a group of men and women, many of whom worked in the helping professions. My co-leader and I noticed that when the women were crossing the stream over rocks, at the very first moment of hesitation, men would reach out to give support and lead the women across. While a few women replied with "No, thanks, I'm fine," others seemed to leap at the chance of being rescued.

While this was a generous act on the men's part, it also blocked the struggle that would have enabled most of these women to rely on themselves. The group had signed on for a "wilderness within" adventure in which they would test their limits. To use everyday chivalry at this point would have prevented the women knowing they could make it themselves.

We decided to talk with the group about their helpful support. We discussed the challenges of women relying on themselves physically and of men allowing themselves not to be overly protective. The men admitted that they never seemed to protect one another. The men and women had no idea of what they were doing. It all came naturally as a result of socialization in childhood.

These gender differences permeate our everyday lives. Mark Suwyn, whom I discussed in the last chapter, told about a discovery he'd recently made. When women executives came into his office, he would open mail, answer telephone calls, and shuffle papers. When a man entered, he turned off his telephone and listened attentively. Mark said he had never realized the connection between his present-day behavior and his childhood learning. A simple example was at dinnertime. When his mother called the children for dinner, they ignored her repeated calls. When his father called just one time, they ran inside. Mark said it had taken him years to change his attitude.

Indeed, as adults we can consciously choose to make changes. When my friend Dick and I have dinner together, we begin each conversation with the mutual understanding "I talk, you talk." Our dinners last as long as my longest dinners with my women friends. I think for many years people have assumed that women own the domain of close friendship, and at times feel morally superior about it.

Women, from girlhood on, have been socialized to give and seek emotional support. They often sponge up the unexpressed feelings of men. Morris Taggert, a friend and colleague, once reminded me that when women carry the emotions for the men in their family and work systems—and have low expectations of them—they are letting men off the hook from doing the emotional growth work they need to do. This was a timely reminder for me that we often unconsciously strip others of the dignity of their own learning experiences. At the same time, women need to realize that male partners will not always give the same quality of emotional intimacy in friendship that their women friends give.

I have heard several men express jealousy about the closeness between women. I suggest they remember the cardinal rule. "Empathy before strategy." They say they feel inadequate. My question to my male clients is always the same: "Are you willing to be a learner?" Then I remind them that they grew up in a culture in which men who were expressive were labeled as weak.

For men and women alike, seeking support is important in deepening commitments. There are different realms in which support can be found: within the family, with friends, and at work. Let's look at these individually to see how reaching out can enrich our lives.

Family as Support

When I reflect on my own family support, I realize how much I have expanded my thinking about family.

At this age I no longer take my family of origin for granted. The importance of loved ones was brought home when my brother died suddenly at age fifty-eight of a heart attack. None of us had had a chance to say good-bye, and we regretted our assumption that strong and steadfast Bob would always be there. In fact, since our mom and dad had died at ages seventy-six and eighty-four, respectively, we were all assuming we'd live as long. The impact of a sibling death touched me more deeply—probably because we were of the same generation. At the end of Bob's funeral, my four remaining siblings and I moved toward one another and formed a circle. We stood looking into one another's faces in silence. I wondered if they were asking what I was asking: "Who is next?" Since Bob's death, we no longer take our relationships for granted. We show up for one another, and our closeness grows.

The American ethic of self-reliance does not serve us well in this crucial area of support. Other cultures around the world stress family ties to a much greater degree, as can be seen in this telling example.

When I was trekking in Tanzania, I learned that a seven-year-old daughter of one of our local guides, Richard, needed medical attention that she was unable to get in the bush. She had been living for six years with involuntary spitting up, which came upon her suddenly and daily. Doctors there said she would need a pediatrician's help, available only in Nairobi. Since I had lectured there, I had contacts and immediately made some calls and arranged for the child to get help. I not only arranged an appointment with a Nairobi pediatrician but also arranged for housing for the parents and daughter and the necessary papers at the border. When I followed up later, I learned that the family had not yet gone. They were unable to cross the border because they showed up in a group of thirteen. When I said family, Richard thought family as he knew it. It was some time before Richard and his family were able to cross into Kenya.

This was a dramatic contrast to my family's injunction: "You do it yourself." This was not to say that support was lacking. My parents gave support through traditional patterns—for example, sewing clothes, cooking our favorite foods, and supporting our school interests. Dad, especially, supported our world of ideas. For emotional support, I turned to Gram and my sister Sue, my favorite listeners.

As I reflect on my own parenting, I am much more forgiving and accepting of my parents. I think one of the most humbling parenting experiences is to look back and recognize our failings and mistakes. I wince painfully when I think of times when I thought I was being supportive of my children and learned later that they had not felt the same way.

When I left the suburbs to move into the city after my divorce, my daughter, Jeanine, transferred to a school environment very different from the one she knew. She witnessed fighting, kicking, and bullying, and became quite fearful and cautious. When she attempted to discuss her feelings with me, I would logically explain the situation and try to help her understand what lay under the behavior rather than support her feelings about the incident. She simply needed empathy.

When I learned one day that I needed a surgical procedure, I knew I should call my son, Jerry, who was out East at school, but it was exam week. To be supportive from my perspective was to withhold the news. I felt protective. With friends' encouragement and nudging, though, I called him. "This is really hard for me, but I have to tell you that I have to have some minor surgery. Ninety-nine percent of me does not want to tell you. I want to protect you." "Protect me!" he exclaimed. "Mom, why do you call that protection? When you don't tell me what's going on with you, I feel ripped off—cheated. Why don't you treat me like an adult? I have a right to know what is happening in your life." I had not realized how disrespectful it was to withhold this information. I realized, much later, that it also blocked his caring for me.

Just because parents may not have been supportive in early years does not mean that we do not learn along the way to make changes. Take Lonnie, for instance. She was the second daughter in a family of two girls and two boys. Her sister, who was only fourteen months older, was clearly her father's favorite. Lonnie felt support from her mother and brothers, but she often felt like a lonely outsider in the presence of her dominating father. She married young to leave home and cut herself off from her family entirely except for infrequent contact with her divorced parents.

Early in Lonnie's marriage, her husband, Mike, started beating her. She stayed, terrified, because of his threats to make it worse. She kept her car keys on her body at all times and parked her car in the driveway away from the garage, ready for a quick exit. A year later, Lonnie went to see an attorney who told her to just walk. She decided to take his advice and planned to leave the next morning. That evening she called her father, whom she had not seen in fifteen years, to tell him she was leaving.

After Mike left for work, she packed a few personal things. She was terrified that he might return before she left the house. The doorbell rang. "Oh, my God, he's back!" she thought. "He forgot something." Trembling in panic, she went to the door. There, crowded into the entryway, stood her entire family—her parents and her sister and two brothers. They had driven nonstop across three states through the night to be there for her. Lonnie burst into tears at the sight and said that for the first time in her life she felt total unconditional support.

Often we hold on to old photos in our minds of our family members, forgetting that these people too are capable of changing and growing. While Lonnie was surprised with her family's changes, Sarah, another client, was able to be closely involved in her mother's support changing.

Sarah, an elementary school music teacher, was a client of mine. Her mother, Jewel, had pretended to be accepting when Sarah announced shortly after her divorce that she was lesbian. Jewel did not know what to do with the information. Later, when Sarah said, "I'm a lesbian," her mother turned to her and said crisply, "No, you're not! And what about the children?" Sarah promised her mother that she was thinking carefully about how to tell her children, ages twelve, ten, and eight.

When Jewel met Sarah's new partner, Jackie, reality set in

and she did not know where to turn. Jewel said that her generation had kept this kind of information secret and that at times she wished this had not changed. Jewel was a prominent leader in her conservative synagogue, and cultural prohibitions blocked her from having a friend with whom she felt close enough to disclose her new secret.

With Sarah's encouragement, Jewel courageously decided to risk attending a support group for families of lesbians and gays. Jewel was surprised to recognize how comfortable she was there. She met other parents who could support her feelings. "They were all so kind and accepting," she reported. It did not take long before Jewel attended meetings on a regular basis—with her grandchildren—and became a strong advocate for her "re-formed" family.

Jewel became increasingly indignant about stereotyping and judgmentalism as she grew to know the families better. She asked one day, "How dare society make a judgment when there are more than two million gay mothers and fathers in America and more than ten thousand lesbians have borne children through sperm donation?"

Sarah was fortunate; her mother did a total shift and became a spokesperson for all gay and lesbian families. This story may sound simple, given what appears to be an ideal ending, but what I have not mentioned is that Sarah's brother and sister have still not acknowledged their sister's relationship with Jackie and remain cut off to this day. In the meantime, Sarah and her new family are creating new rituals, even though the "first family" still chooses to be cut off.

Support of Friends

Much of my support comes through my friendship family, which is made up of several couples and men and women friends I call my "family of affiliation." I share life rituals with these friends and rely on their caring about my family and me. Since my blood kin live far away, I have learned to rely heavily on my friendship family for support. All our children are a part of this expanded family.

When my son was preparing his wedding invitation list, he commented on the richness of sitting down and listing those who had supported him throughout the years. My friendships have taught me how much I can learn about support.

I recently listened to a friend who did not receive a particular telephone call from a man. She began to say, "I think it's because I am too old and too fat." At that point I cut her off and jumped in to protest, loyally, "But that is about him; you are lovely, and—" at which point my friend strongly interrupted, "Wait, wait. I am asking you to hear me; please just listen to my feelings." In my attempt to support her and because I see her beauty fully, I wanted to change her feelings. She taught me what she needed at the time; I learned what felt supportive to her and how difficult it can be at times to get the support we need.

As we have seen, men have trouble seeking support. Ron, with whom I was doing some individual coaching, had bought into the male myth of not needing support. When I told him it was essential to tell at least one person his secret that he had brain cancer, he could not think of a single man to tell. Ron eventually thought of a man and came back to report that his friend had many secrets to share with him as well. They began having dinner together every two weeks. As Ron felt safe with his friend, he was free to think out loud.

Morris Taggart engages in "committed conversations" with several friends, both male and female. These conversations reflect that we can become more fully known to one another and assume that the dialogue will be ongoing in our commitment to deepening honesty in friendship. These friendships outside primary relationships enrich paired relationships and marriages. I recall telling a good man friend one night at dinner how much I appreciated his friendship and the fresh thinking he brought to the table. I added some comment about being single and how important my friendships were to me. He replied, "I too need support from outside my marriage, so my friendships with you and others enrich what I bring to my marriage." The assumption here is that his marriage is strong and honest enough that he sees this as a true asset.

Support does not always have to come from friends. Who among us does not know someone who has joined a support group dealing with chronic illness, consciousness-raising, alcoholism, or life changes? When the twelve-step movement became the fastest-growing social movement in the United States during the 1980s, I think it offered safe support settings because of the focus on anonymity, honest expression of feelings, and confidentiality. Groups offer plain human energy in their caring.

Support and Work

Many of my clients, men and women, talk about how difficult it is to recognize support at work. These days I ask them about such support as naturally as I would ask about their workplace.

Bob, age forty-five, in consultation about his career, had tears in his eyes when I asked him about his lonely position as CEO of his company. I reminded him that his corporate rule matched his upbringing: You go it alone and don't need support. He said he thought it weird to feel so isolated while surrounded by thousands of employees. He said, as if to convince himself, "But I really do have support of all kinds here." Finally, he acknowledged that it was paid support, and he was never certain whether the support was genuine or motivated by the giver's ambition for advancement.

He admitted that he was totally confused. He said that in a downsizing environment with consultants roving through the offices, he felt cautious in speaking with his chair of the board who he knew was carefully monitoring his honesty. Bob entered into a support group with other executives who were facing dramatic life changes and seeking to discover who they were beyond their roles. One man's company had been bought by a multinational group and pushed him into early retirement; another had just learned he had colon cancer. A third man had the job of firing two thousand people, and another, after twenty-nine years of employment and having lost three assistants, was on probation to raise his profits. All these events had forced the men to closely examine what they had been committed to and how much of their lives they had forfeited. Bob recognized that he had to learn how to gather support for himself.

Self-reliance

Commitments can be demanding. Like the stock market, they fluctuate in what they give back. Thus we must take responsibility for supporting ourselves in order to sustain vitality in our commitments. I have often commented on the strength of those who have survived horrific situations and become stronger for the experience, but it was years before I personally realized how relevant self-reliance was.

I went on a dog-sledding expedition to the sub-Arctic, a trial expedition with adventurer-explorer Will Steger, who later was to lead the famed expeditions to the North and South poles. We had just flown into Churchill, Manitoba, and, with the sled dogs settled, were setting up camp before going out on the pack ice. In the hardened snow, scrub trees and a few white ptarmigan birds seemed to be the only sign of tundra life. Desirous of an afternoon cup of tea, I expressed my wish to Will. He turned aside for a moment and promptly placed an ax in my hands. I got the message—I was to cut a small tree and chop some wood. First I cleared some snow, then chopped the wood, built a fire, melted snow in a kettle, and finally added teabags. After this ninety-minute endeavor, I wearily sat down to the most satisfying cup of tea I have ever tasted! For months after my return, I smiled in appreciation as I turned on my automatic stove.

Another form of support for me is the great outdoors. Recently I was writing in a friend's cabin in northern Wisconsin when I realized how grounding Mother Nature is for me. In the morning, dancing winds moved through my writing room, accompanied by sounds of rustling pine needles and shimmering birch leaves. The loons added their calls and seemed to stop self-consciously when I started to write about them.

When I cannot be in the out-of-doors, I am surrounded in my study with pictures that conjure memories from the slides in my mind. As I take in these sounds and images and fresh air, I feel more connected to the natural world—and to my natural self. I feel a part of the whole.

Support—friendship, marriages, family, work, community organizations, and loved ones—sustains our commitments. With support we can ask larger questions, hear challenges, make adaptive changes, while staying connected. We can go deeper into our commitments and accept new commitments in our rapidly changing world. Most important, we can further develop our lives of commitment to our next generations and to our society—with purpose and meaning.

When I come home from a long day and pick up my telephone messages, I press my "saved messages" button on my telephone. The first message I hear is from my granddaughter Morgan Elizabeth: "Hi, Ama. Be right over, Ama." My heart fills, my shoulders relax, and everything seems to fall into place. I know what matters. I am connected.

Chapter 5

Endurance: Staying with the Experience

"The thought that we are enduring the unendurable is one of the things that keep us going." —Molly Haskell

MT. ELBRUS, USSR MOUNTAINEERING CAMP, THE CAUCASUS MOUNTAINS. *This has been one of the hardest days of my life. I can hardly breathe at this altitude; my body aches. I thought I might have altitude sickness. What a contrast to my high spirits this morning, when we began our ascent in crisp snow and dazzling sunlight. Given its 22,000-foot peak, I can see why climbers train here for Mt. Everest! Our climb brought us to the Preihut at the 13,500-foot saddle of Mt. Elbrus. Mountain huts, placed at varying distances for hikers and trekkers, are usually made of wood or stone. The "hut" is hardly a hut; it looks like a giant loaf of steel bread glimmering in the sun.*

Feeling the effects of the altitude early in the day, we paced ourselves slowly. We practiced the Himalayan resting step all the way, settling all our weight on our bones before planting the next foot forward, like young children climbing stairs. Suddenly the fickle weather shifted boldly. The wind was fierce; our ultra-light synthetic clothing felt skimpy against its force. My friend Iris, in her bright yellow rain pants, watched despairingly as the cold froze her pants and the wind tore them to shreds. Eyelashes froze; eyes teared up. Wherever our facial skin was exposed, we saw frosty hairs. I was grateful for my balaclava face mask! As the snow slapped at us through the climb, I privately longed to retreat.

I'd never before realized how slowly one can move and still make progress. I recited my favorite climbing mantra: "No goal is too difficult if we climb with care and confidence." We took the space necessary for silence. I recalled our Russian head mountaineer's thickly accented question: "Mason, vat is your goal?" as we went off on our preparatory hikes. Was our goal to be this miserable, this cold and chilled, and sick on top of it? I muttered, "Is this what we have been training to do—endure misery?" We had brought our tents, cooking gear, and food with us from the States so that we could backpack in the mountains. The Russians had refused to let us go off on our own, because an avalanche had just killed two hundred people. "Yet they would let us come this close to freezing to death on the mountain!" I muttered.

When we arrived at the hut, a three-story structure that holds about twelve people, we faced more agony. It was extremely cold. We were exhausted, but we had been warned not to sleep when chilled and nauseous because of possible altitude mountain sickness. Iris and I attempted to go down the mountainside to the outhouse. This involved a steep walk that seemed long in the sharp, biting wind. We entered another rounded steel shed with a hole in the ice for a toilet. When the toilet tissue caught in the updraft and blew back up in our faces, we decided to improvise. We returned to the hut and used large plastic garbage bags for "indoor toilets."

Iris, Kathy, and I felt as if we were being held hostage by our nausea and headaches. We agreed that if it had been any earlier, we would have attempted to descend. I thought back to the time when the guides had offered us pastries and vodka at a rest hut—something unheard of in America. I wondered if this repast had contributed to my queasiness and decided that perhaps in the Caucasus, climbers have to numb themselves to survive.

We busied ourselves by cooking potatoes and canned meat for dinner. Our guide told us that another group of climbers was descending from the summit. We knew they would be hungry and depleted, and cooking would give us something to do. Cooking was *laborious; everything slows down at this altitude! When the climbers returned, we listened over dinner to their stories of the ascent.*

We went to bed soon after dinner. To generate extra body heat, we pulled our wool hats down over our heads and arranged our sleeping bags in a row. Our mountain guide, Vladimir, joined us. We remained wide awake; the wind continued to howl. Snuggling together side by side for warmth comforted me, but the euphoria of the early morning was long forgotten.

We started down the mountain early the next morning. Surprisingly, within hours of arriving at the base we were able to look back on the experience and acknowledge the beauty, the adventure, the high satisfaction of completing our climb. The frozen moments melted with time.

A photograph I keep in my study is a reminder of the almost mystical beauty of that shimmering snow-rock world. No trace of our pain is evident. We had endured! Iris and I laughed as we teased each other about how we had chosen this experience and paid good money to endure. I know that each climb becomes a part of our history, a part of our stories, and a part of us.

The lesson on Mt. Elbrus was endurance. The climb required that we not give up. During the climb we faced our doubts and our wavering stamina, but we continued on.

Tenacity is the cement for any commitment. I often seek endurance challenges intentionally, and have asked myself why I have this hunger. I like to test my stamina, my endurance, through adventures. There is a deep satisfaction in knowing that I have endured another challenge. It is the same with people I've led. Whether my clients are upper-middle-class or blue-collar, we find we're all equal on the rocks. I often tell clients on my Journeys Inward adventures, "The trip is three weeks, but it will last forever." I think this is why so many more people seek adventure travel vacations, despite their discomfort and often arduous physical challenges.

Staying Power

Most of us know stories of people whose courage astounds us. These people never make the news; they are everyday heroes. Some experience involuntary adventures— surviving during an earthquake or some other natural disaster. Others take a stand for their values by picketing, demonstrating, or writing letters to editors, or speaking up at public shareholders' meetings.

I remember the payoff in endurance in the Nestlé boycott in the 1980s. When Americans learned that Nestlé's introduction of inferior infant formula to a poverty-stricken area of the world had resulted in the starvation of many thousands of children, groups began to picket supermarkets that sold Nestlé products. In response to petitions, pamphlets, and upset citizens' boycotting of products, Nestlé finally dropped their infant-formula business in Africa.

We probably all know people who have made such total investments in their commitments that they seem unaware of how remarkable it looks to others. They don't seem to count the costs. They have the staying power that is intrinsic to endurance—carrying a heavy load while standing tall.

Joe Selvaggio is a paragon of staying power. Joe, a former priest, has persevered in developing an inner-city project called Project for Pride in Living (PPL) in Minneapolis, now in its twenty-fifth year, in which he "teaches people how to fish." Through his community-supported programs, groups from many diverse neighborhoods work together to rebuild homes, renovate neighborhoods, start small businesses, and restore community spirit. PPL works with about two hundred families at a time. Joe brings together people from all classes and races to work in their commitment to change a neighborhood and quality of living.

There is a book about Joe entitled *Until All Are Housed in Dignity*. Joe tells the story of a family with twelve children who not only worked toward owning their own home but now have all the skills needed to maintain it, thanks to PPL's Self-Sufficiency Programs. After families complete the Self-Sufficiency Programs, which take between six months to five years, they attend a graduation ceremony in which they receive an award. Joe said that through involvement in PPL, families moving into crack- and crime-ridden areas become involved in and committed to their new neighborhoods, and slowly bring about change.

I asked Joe what sustained his commitment. He said, "I used to say I would give five years of my life and then be a 'normal' person, but I can't do that." He said his investment has gone beyond habit. "Each day brings new light and new energy," he said. His life is a testament to commitment.

Commitments often grow out of society's needs. A recent example of endurance has been the commitment of HIV-infected patients and their care givers. Recently I attended a fund-raising dinner for the Aliveness Project in Minneapolis, a drop-in center for those living with HIV or AIDS. Although somewhat resistant when my friend Ethelyn and I arrived at this old building in a rather unsafe neighborhood, I tightened my resolve as I thought of my nephew Michael, who had died of AIDS four years ago on that very day. I felt relief at knowing my grief had finally healed enough so that I could be there. I think I also knew that that night would be a part of my healing process.

In the center, the project maintains a food shelf, operates a meals-on-wheels program, and offers counseling, massage, and acupuncture. Run with very little overhead, the organization employs only five paid staff. Remarkably, volunteers donate six hundred hours of their time a month to keep the center going.

When we entered the beautifully decorated meeting hall upstairs, we saw a lovely banquet donated by the Marriott to honor its commitment not to treat HIV-infected people as second-class citizens. Spirits were high.

Throughout the evening, several members and volunteers spoke about their involvement with the project. Some were HIV-infected and knew that they themselves would eventually need the project's services. Some HIV-infected men told stories about how the disease had led them to stop drinking, to seek community, and to take care of themselves in ways they never had before. Ann, an HIV-infected mother, told of the anguish she had endured in wondering whether her daughter would die before she did. After her daughter died of AIDS at age three, Ann developed project resources for women and children. Her endurance was admirable; she remained in the presence of others who were living with HIV. Despite the ever present possibility of burnout, the volunteers work constantly in their commitment to battle this epidemic. That evening reinforced the endurance of the HIV-infected as well as the caregivers. Those who spoke agreed that they receive much more than they give.

That night's event tapped my awareness of endurance. I felt my compassion for others at a deeper level, and I realized that thinking globally and acting locally not only can make a difference in people's lives but also can ignite the spirit. We read the stories of those who live committed lives with purpose, people usefully engaged with others in meaningful commitments. The endurance of those in the Aliveness Project, for example, not only unites our communities but inspires hope for all of us. Their staying power is remarkable.

Perhaps one of the greatest examples of staying power is the story of the Dalai Lama and other Tibetans who fled after the Chinese invaded their homeland in 1959 and destroyed more than six thousand monasteries. More than 1.2 million Tibetans, one fifth of the population, have died as a result of execution, torture, and starvation. Through their endurance they have established a government in exile in India. Perhaps what is most remarkable about the Dalai Lama, the recipient of the 1993 Nobel Peace Prize, is his compassion concerning the long-lasting cultural upheaval. His belief in nonviolence still holds, despite all the human rights violations.

Endurance is indeed important to social action, but it plays a vital role in our private lives as well. Foremost among the bonds we make is that of matrimony. Since, as we all know, marriages have their ups and downs, the ability to endure the hard times becomes a point of pride for many couples. A touching illustration can be seen in some friends of mine.

My friends Ethelyn and Howard, who have been married thirty-eight years, were vacationing in the Badlands of South Dakota, where dried, crusted earth and rocks in deep hues blanket the earth. Ethelyn exclaimed as she looked at delicate flowers pushing their way up through the rock, "Look, Howard, at the tenacity of those flowers!" He put his arm around her and replied, "You and me, Eth, looking at those flowers together—that is tenacity!"

We often do not see our own staying power until we look back over the years. The story of Clarice, a woman who was on a search, illustrates how endurance will carry us.

Clarice had been struggling in therapy with issues of abandonment. She had a crusty exterior and managed quite successfully to distance herself from others. At age sixty-one, she said she wanted to get serious about her life. Clarice seemed steeped in guilt, but her pain was clearly most intense when she spoke about abandonment and self-hate.

Clarice told stories of her parents' sending her off to live with her grandparents from age two to four. She was told that her mother had to work at the canteen on the military base. Her parents had placed her five-year-old brother in an institution without saying what was wrong. Clarice knew Eddy had had learning problems. Their parents never told the other children they were sending Eddy away; the family visited him only one time—in the first year. Clarice said her parents never mentioned his name or what had happened to

Eddy throughout their lives. She was steeped in guilt and shame, since she was closest to Eddy.

Her role in the family had been to "big-sister" him. As a very young girl, she would read to her brother and write his name on a slate, hoping he would learn to do the same. She worked daily, tirelessly, and angrily to push him to write his own name. She said she hated the little girl she had been because of her failure to save her brother from being institutionalized. Her parents repeatedly said, "Forget Eddy." At the time she dared not talk with anyone about it; she feared she too might "disappear." She felt very responsible for Eddy. In adulthood, her self-hatred was directly linked to the fact that she too had abandoned her brother.

Clarice sounded like a tearful, anxious parent when she spoke about Eddy. I gently reminded her that seven-year-olds typically follow very loyally the unspoken messages and implicit rules of their families and that there was nothing she could have done to help Eddy. I encouraged her to have some compassion for the seven-year-old and assured her that her parents had abandoned Eddy, not her. She then said that early on she had tried often to trace him to no avail and then gave up. She had waffled throughout the years about whether she should continue her search or not. She did not know whether he was alive or dead, but I reminded her that if he was dead, there would be a record of his death in some institutional archive. Most important, Clarice realized she did not have to forget Eddy. "It was just a family message," she reported. "It was not truth."

One day we decided to telephone the last institution she had checked. When that failed, we called center after center, checking institutional archives. After all, it had been fifty-one years since her parents had taken her brother away. After many dead ends, Clarice finally remembered a name of a facility. We began calling up and down the East Coast, following Eddy's trail. Through a series of contacts we finally found Eddy's case manager. I told her that his sister was with me. She was shocked at first and said, "Why, we gave him a guardian years ago because there was no sign of any kin." She cited the rule that she could not release information to anyone outside the professional circle. Clarice stood beside me while I repeated every sentence Betsy spoke. I then pleaded, "You have to talk with her; she has waited all these years for this moment!" All color drained from Clarice's face.

"But you know, I'm not allowed to do this, don't you?" Betsy queried. She continued, "I cannot release psychological records to her!"

"Don't, then," I said, "just tell her about her brother!"

"Put her on," sighed Betsy.

She told Clarice about Eddy and his Down's syndrome and how lovable and gentle a man he was. She said that he once had made coat hangers but now did woodworking, that he functioned very well and was well liked. She also described Eddy's guardian and how well cared for Eddy was. Clarice, who had not seen her brother for fifty-one years, had found her fifty-eight-year-old brother! Tears streamed down her cheeks; she was overwhelmed by the caring voice at the other end.

That was just the beginning. Clarice began to reconnect with Eddy though letters and photographs before going east. After her first visit, Clarice came in to show me pictures of her brother. She reported that when she spoke with his foster family, they told her that Eddy can write one word—his name! Clarice burst into tears, knowing that what she had taught him so many years ago was still with him. The foster parents also reported that after they showed him a picture of Clarice and her family, Eddy kept coming back to it, saying, "Clarice, Clarice!" Clarice and Eddy are back in each other's lives in a new and wonderful way; Clarice visits him as often as possible.

There are other families in which endurance is quietly lived day by day. Such is the story of Calvin, a state government employee, and Janet, an environmental lobbyist. Janet and Cal decided to keep their physically and mentally disabled child at home. Both parents have careers that take them outside their home. They begin their day with little Sam at 5:30 A.M. when he awakens. Although seven years old, Sam developmentally is a toddler.

For Janet and Cal, placing Sam in an institution was never an option. They knew raising him by themselves would be hard. They knew they would have to make sacrifices—being on duty whenever Sam was awake, struggling to balance their care for him with that for their able-bodied son, and sustaining a willingness to witness Sam's painful struggles with all physical movement. Neither is a martyr. Both are very practical about caring for Sam; they say they "simply have a job to do."

Despite their commitment, there are times when self-doubts surface and they waffle about their decision. "Did we do the right thing? Where will this lead us?" They speak honestly at those times, but also know they are controlling some of their feelings, preserving their energy for their commitment to Sam. They understand that someday they will have very hard decisions to make. They have been told that Sammy will probably not live to adulthood. Neither analyzes very much or pushes to feel more deeply; they need to preserve their emotional energy for parenting Sam. Janet and Cal glow when they tell their stories of Sam and his love and accomplishments. One day they were thrilled to report that he had made a real achievement—he could reach the doorknob in his room and hold on to it.

Their commitment demands that they forfeit many of life's pleasures, since they carry Sam's well-being so responsibly. Yet they are constantly finding ways to balance their endurance with the rest of their world.

The bonds of endurance we form reach far beyond the family, of course. For many people, maintaining their friendships is of paramount importance. Often we can rely more readily on our friendships than our family to support our endurance. Yet these bonds can go even further, as I learned once on one of my outdoor experiences.

Some years ago I was a consultant to a group home for chemically dependent felons who were in recovery. These men had endured difficult childhoods—the majority had been physically or sexually abused as young children. Most had given up prior to coming to the house, but were willing to endure the group/work home in order to maintain their drug and alcohol sobriety. Our contract was to work on healthy sexuality in the context of their relationships. When a few of the men asked me, "Hey, Marilyn, what's a relationship?" I asked their director if we could rock climb instead of talking in seminars. She agreed.

The experience with them on the North Shore of Lake Superior was rich; many of the young men said they had never been in a wilderness setting before. On the first climbing-instruction day, several group members came strutting out, and one of them said, "Hey, cool, man—this is going to be a blast." By noon that day, when we were belaying each other in the climbs, one of the young men became wedged in a deep crevice between two rocks. I heard Roman, tears running down his cheeks, say "Hey, man, I'm scared shitless. How do I get myself out of this mess?" He finally freed himself with the encouragement of others and hugged everyone when he reached the ground.

By risking and pushing themselves in a supportive environment, they exceeded all expectations of themselves. I belayed Lenny, a twenty-two-year-old, from the ground. As soon as he got almost to the top, he faced an overhang—a rock that seems to be leaning over toward you. "Let me down; let me down, dammit!" he exclaimed.

I replied, "You can do it, Lenny. Hang in there; that's what this is all about."

"I can't," he replied. Other voices joined mine in encouraging him. Lenny became rageful. "Okay, have it your way. I'm going to untie my rope. You *have* to let me down."

I responded, "Lenny, I will certainly lower you, but there are two requirements. First, you have to give it the greatest shot you can, and second, you cannot talk abusively to me." I was terrified and looked up at Bill, who was working the top of the climb, wondering if I was making a mistake. Then Lenny, sputtering and groaning, made two sudden giant leaps forward, threw his entire shoulder over the rock, and pulled himself to the top. Cheers and hoots came from the rest of the group. After Lenny rapelled down, he sauntered slowly over to me. Shuffling his feet in the dirt, with eyes to the ground, he haltingly said, "Uh, I guess I really made it tough for you. I want you to know how much I appreciated your hanging in with me." I thanked Lenny and reminded him that he was the one who endured the climb.

By the time the group returned to the group home, they had decided that all the other men in the program should also have a climbing experience. Knowing that grant money was no longer available, the men organized a project of painting houses and washing cars to raise money so that others in the program could go to the North Shore. They did not give up. They had learned a lesson in how to endure.

I see clients who are facing substance abuse, multiple affairs, early-onset Alzheimer's disease, or battering. I have worked with clients who have learned that as their spouse's untreated alcoholism progresses, they naturally distance themselves from the once primary relationship. In this process there is a shift from unconditional to conditional commitments. I think any of us who has lived with such struggles can truly understand that endurance is not always the most healthy trait. Endurance carried too far has negative consequences. Such is Fred's story.

Fred, a thirty-eight-year-old wiry, highly energetic consultant, was truly a long-distance runner. His ability to endure carried into his work; he seemed able to tolerate the long hours and lack of sleep his work required. One day when he arrived home from a business trip, his six-year-old son ran to meet him, as he typically did. When they entered the house, Fred's son proudly showed him his new drawing from school, which was taped onto the refrigerator door. Fred smiled as he approached. He narrowed his eyes as he saw two figures—his son and his mother. "They asked us to draw our family in school today." Fred said he felt a pain never felt before, from deep within. When he came to see me, he had made the decision to leave his ninety-hour-a-week job and to take a different job within the company. Fred did recommit to his family and now tells his story to other young co-workers who carried endurance too far.

I learned of another story of endurance denied. Only in this example it is the parents who are attempting to protect their adult children from enduring hardship of any kind.

A few years ago I was invited to do a television show in San Francisco on which, as the guest psychologist, I was to respond to the issue of young men moving back home. The station had asked three pairs of mothers and sons to be on the show. They never thought to include the fathers. The program was based on a front-page article in the *New York Times* that revealed that 32 percent of men between 26 and 32 were moving back home, compared with only 20 percent of women in that age group.

In each case, the son had taken over his parents' home. The parents of one were living in a backyard trailer house. In another case, the parents had given up their retirement travel plans because of their increased financial burden. What stood out most clearly to me was the fact that the mothers had become voluntary hostages, giving their power to their adult children. While I realize that some adult children move home for educational support, I think many are part of a system of denial that is harmful in the long run.

In contrast, endurance can also exist in the form of denial that does not mean self-sacrifice. Rather, denial is often the psychological buffer that comes as nature's caring way to protect us from the pain of our struggles because we are too young, not ready, or could not survive.

Lindsay had survived a traumatic full-body injury after a car accident and was living a rich, productive life when I met her. Her speech had been affected, yet she had worked for years with a speech therapist and now spoke clearly. When I asked her what helped her survive, she replied, "Why, denial, of course. I simply could not have borne it all without denial." She went on to describe how she had put on hold the emotional trauma of being disfigured, physically disabled below the waist, and speech-impaired. Lindsay said learning to walk and speak again had taken years of physical therapy. When her healing was advanced enough, she was able to enter into therapy to work through the emotional trauma she had experienced.

Andy, an olive-skinned, dark-haired man of stocky build, struggled to make his decision to leave his job as CEO of a large corporation. He had discovered the chair of the board led the meetings in ways that paralleled Andy's verbally abusive family of origin. The chair would make shaming comments like: "When are you going to get balls, Andy, and get this company moving?" For several years he had been numb to how naturally he could endure verbal abuse. He grappled for over a year with his decision to say no to belonging to his company's inner circle of power and money.

Andy was weary from the tension and from living the "corporate affair marriage"—a marriage in which the corporation, like an outside lover, could pull Andy away from his wife at a moment's notice. Finally, a home scene tipped the scales for him.

When Andy left town for a business conference, his wife, Ruth, and sons sat on their back porch watching some birds after she picked the children up from the sitter's after her work day. The eldest son, eight years old, said "Mommy, I

don't think I want to go into business like Daddy did."
"Why not?" his mother asked. "Because I think I would
want to spend more time with my kids." When Ruth told
Andy this story, he decided he needed to leave. He had
become aware of what really mattered.

Andy confronted the chair about the abuse and said he
was concerned about its effects on the entire organization.
Yet the chair responded in silence. Andy felt better about
himself, even though he did not feel heard. As he began his
termination, he gathered support from men outside the
organization who had made similar decisions.

Today Andy is very satisfied with his work in the publishing field, which allows him to live a lifestyle that fits his
family's values. Andy said he now likes himself much better
and, for the first time, can feel a sense of integrity.

The Light of Endurance

A person's willingness to stay the course can inspire us all.
When my friend Iris and I went to Tibet, we carried along
the book *My Journey to Lhasa*. The author, Alexandra David-
Neel, was a philosopher and journalist who had studied
Tibetan Buddhism and the Tibetan language to prepare for
her journey into Lhasa, Tibet, in 1924 at age fifty-four.
Alexandra was a frustrated student at the Sorbonne who
struggled to find her own way; she was lured by the
unknown. She devoted her studies to Eastern religions and
folklore and felt a oneness with a large statue of Buddha in
the Musée Guimet. She continued studies in journalism and
music as well, but her passionate commitment to Tibetan
Buddhism remained strong. She went to great lengths to
experience both the mundane and the extraordinary. Her
commitment sealed her story of her exceptional physical and
mental endurance in crossing the peaks and rivers of the
Himalayas posing as a beggar. She became the first Western

woman to enter the forbidden holy city of Lhasa and to meet the Dalai Lama. "I had endeavored to reach the Tibetan capital rather because I had been challenged than out of any real desire to visit it."

She continued her passionate relationship with Tibet and Tibetan Buddhism throughout her entire life and died at the age of 101, surrounded by her simple Tibetan artifacts in a small home in Digne, France.

We can't all show such steadfastness. For most of us, endurance is shown in smaller, everyday ways. I never will forget the day a few years ago when I was biking up a mountainside in Arizona. As I neared the top, exhausted from the eight miles' uphill effort, I pedaled so slowly that I felt it would be quicker to walk. Just at that moment, a ninety-year-old man, walking up the mountain, appeared at my side. He was walking at the same pace I was bicycling. He said he walks up the mountain three times a week.

Whether passion-driven or family-given, whether for community causes or crisis-induced, our endurance, our capacity to hang in for the long haul, is what will provide the base for a society in which we tighten the threads of the fabric of the meaning of commitment.

Chapter 6

The Crux: The Crucial Choice

"You must do the thing you think you cannot do."
—Eleanor Roosevelt

DEVIL'S TOWER, WYOMING. *It was clear and still this morning when we awoke at the base of Devil's Tower. I did not need to awake; I had not slept. I had been too anxious, too excited to sleep; the big climb awaited me. From my sleeping bag, I looked up at the rock monolith, with its 5,117-foot summit towering above the tall mass of columns rising out of the talus and rubble, and recalled an ancient Sioux legend I had just recently learned.*

In the legend, several young girls are trying to escape a bear. In response to the girls' prayer, the stone spirits push the rocks high into the sky. The rocks are so close to the sky that they become the seven stars of the Pleiades. As the bear claws at the rocks, trying to reach the girls, it leaves the deeply ridged lines that today are the columns themselves. Try as the bear might, the girls are safe on the Tower formed by the stone spirits.

I lay there hoping the stone spirits would be with me. Painful memories of last year's down-climb here flooded my mind. I could still hear my friend Rolf's words ringing in my ears: "There's no turning back, Marilyn, when you've committed to the climb." Yet I had turned back—after the first pitch. I felt like a lifetime of humiliation had suffused me in that down-climb. Still, I never regretted that experience; I learned far more from down-climbing than I ever had from any ascent! But I did not need to reexperience those negative feelings. Not today.

I was jittery, on edge. Accompanied by three friends, I had returned to the Tower to "go it again." Thankfully, no one said a word about last year's climb; I needed to leave it behind. We moved quietly, efficiently, knowing we wanted to be at the base of the climb before 6:30 a.m. To get there, we had to climb about three hundred feet of large boulders, the talus. We knew it would be a long day, since the Durrance Route with its compelling, dramatic scenery was popular.

We moved steadily up the talus. I felt confident. When we arrived at the base of the climb, I looked up and was flooded with fear. "Damn!" My mouth became dry as waves of fear overtook me. "Am I going to down-climb again?" I asked myself. I did feel prepared for the climb this time, and unlike last year, the weather was in my favor.

While I stood frozen, Will climbed with his usual confidence, trailing his belay rope behind him, to the flat top of the first pitch, named the Leaning Column because of its resemblance to a broken ancient Grecian column. Will called down, "On belay," to signify that he was anchored at the top and was ready for me to tie in and climb. Shakily, I tied the rope into my carabiners, retied my boots, and adjusted my helmet. I knew the moment had come. Joe checked my knots, a part of our routine safety check with each other, and gave me a warm hug. "You can do it," he said calmly. I knew that standing still too long would not help; I just had to take my fear along. Will called, "Climb!" I breathed deeply, closed my eyes for a few seconds, and called, "Climbing!"

Unlike my last climb, I moved steadily, slowly making my way up the column. Suddenly I fell; I cried out, "Falling"—as if Will, who held me at the rope's end, couldn't feel it! As I scrambled to find a stable foothold, I felt Will tighten his hold on the rope; I felt secure. I really trusted Will. If only I trusted myself as much! Below me, Joe and Alan called up in encouragement: "You can do it; keep right on. You're doing fine!" It worked; somehow that energy from beneath me helped. I knew they were there for me.

It wasn't too long before I had completed the first pitch. Will smiled as he welcomed me to the truncated column top. I heaved a sigh of relief, remembering that a year ago I had flung my aching body over the top, only to find I had to be lowered for my down-climb.

When I looked at the second pitch, the seventy-foot, steep Durrance crack, I recalled Rolf's words from the year before: "This next pitch is twice as hard, Marilyn." Then I heard Will's voice encouraging me. I knew I had to stay with the experience and move on.

A climbing instructor from Wyoming with whom we had visited on the talus teasingly called out, "You know, Marilyn, girls can't climb!" It worked. Like an ignited missile, I took off. I moved in steady defiance up the second pitch. I quickly moved beyond my crux. I felt strong and confident when I arrived at the top of the column, laughing with the others about how the friendly taunting had motivated me.

Still, I knew that while I had moved beyond my personal crux, the Tower's crux awaited me. The four of us made our way slowly up the columns, taking turns belaying one another up chimneys and cracks.

Then I saw it. The crux—the crucial point in the climb. We were at the fifth pitch and had to make a move that appeared impossible. It looked as though we would step off into the air—and fall straight down the rock face. The crux involved making a traverse, or lateral, move. The end point of the move, the leap, was not visible, which made belaying almost impossible. Joe explained there was no other way to the top. You just "went for it."

I stared over at the crux, as if by staring long enough a foothold and handhold would appear. I knew enough not to continue this fantasy. I had to make a crucial choice: Either I go for it or I create a severe hardship for the group by asking them to let me rappel from this height and delay other climbers. I had come too far; it was too late to turn back. I wasn't at all sure that my legs were long enough to make the move. I had to trust the unknown, that I would find a handhold and foothold. Joe called, "Trust me; they are there!" I extended my leg as far over as I could. My legs had not attempted a stretch like this since childhood acrobatics classes. I landed on the foothold and simultaneously grabbed the handhold. I had done it! I trusted the unknown in the crux, and it worked.

Afterward, I was able to look down and see the giant shadow the Tower cast on the ground below. The view was breathtaking. And as I looked up, I saw many new possibilities on the route. We scrambled on up. When I saw the flattened top area, I lunged, thrusting my arms forward, longing to be horizontal. In my combined eagerness and desperation, I threw myself into a cactus-like plant that buried its stickers deep into my hands.

Despite my stinging hands and fatigue, I was elated. We took time for pictures, M&Ms, fresh water, and oranges. The sun had shifted. We signed our names in the register and prepared for the long rappel to the base. I was overcome by joy and exhaustion.

Back on the ground, I concluded that while last year's attempt had taught me the valuable lesson of down-climbing, this year's climb had also involved a lesson. I had learned to face a crux and move through it. I now regard my down-climb as a personal achievement for trusting myself to make a wise and difficult decision. Both climbs were a success, for each had provided me an edge.

Someone later asked why I had returned to Devil's Tower. I responded that I had unfinished business. Like most of us, I was guilty of focusing only on the negative—flaws, shame, and failure. I wanted to prove to myself that I could have a positive experience at the Tower. I was curious to see whether I was as prepared as I felt I was.

After the Tower climb, I opened a drawer of memories and named my cruxes: my marriage, my decision to leave a secure teaching position, and my dilemmas in parenting and in several intimate relationships. Now I can see the full benefits in facing cruxes—down-climbing or moving beyond to redefine the relationship. On the rock, I faced the crux concretely and immediately. In my personal life, I got a signal, a moment of knowing.

This signal is a jolting awareness, an initial glimpse, of seeing something we have never seen before, of hearing something in a different way. This moment awakens us to a secret buried deep within our unconscious.

I remember a movie scene in which a man is sitting across from his wife in a restaurant. His moment of knowing came when the egg salad in her sandwich oozed through her teeth as she spoke. This was the moment when he let himself feel his strong reactions—not just to the repugnance he felt when she ate but also to the upsetting moments in their marriage. This egg salad scene merely symbolized years of neglected feelings. Buried emotions, like vegetables long forgotten in the back of the refrigerator, rot over time, and the smell eventually becomes so terrible that we are compelled to do something about them.

We use this moment as a time to assess and either ask for change or end the commitment. Although pivotal, a moment of knowing does not require or guarantee action. It can be a growth point or a stuck point. We use these moments to comment on reality, search for feelings, and accept that the answers lie in our heart, not our head.

Divorce: Get Out—Or Stay In?

"How do you know whether to get out—or stay in?" was my early working title for this book. Divorce statistics have led many to conclude that "Americans don't commit." I think most of us do commit, and whether we commit for the right or wrong reasons, we do face our crucial choices, our cruxes. Moreover, we want to be intentional about the choices we make.

A good example of this concerns Ned, a midlife advertising executive, and Liz, a homemaker and real estate agent. They had first come to see me because their years of personal-growth seminars had seemingly effected no lasting changes. By society's standards of responsibility to family and community, both lived highly committed lives. Yet both said they felt empty.

In her early years Liz had been committed to a beautiful house, children, and community. She was now focused on spiritual growth and "going natural." She stopped shaving her underarms and legs and let her grayish white hair grow long. In addition, she chose flowing Eastern garb as her everyday costume as a way of joining her spirituality group. These changes proved a challenge to Ned, who remained committed to his traditional role as corporate executive and primary breadwinner.

After thirty-one years of marriage, Liz and Ned faced a crux. When they came to see me, Ned was very angry. He had been on business in San Francisco, and Liz had flown in to join him at an important corporate party. "When I saw her walk into that cocktail party wearing her Indian costume with her ringed toes poking through her strap sandals, that was it!" He continued, "I've had it! I thought she would care enough about this big event to dress in her regular clothes. For God's sake, she knows the rules. She intentionally wanted to hurt me; her behavior was really hostile. I am ready to end this marriage." I replied, "Sure, you're entitled to end the marriage, but let's first see if you were ever really committed before you act on this." Ned's moment of knowing led to a year of therapy in which the two learned emotional honesty and for the first time truly knew each other. Liz and Ned have both become involved in a couples spirituality group. Liz has modified her dress, and both have been willing to make the necessary changes to let each other know how much they matter.

Most moments of knowing are more commonplace. I see them in the revelation of a partner's sexual affair, worsening addiction, or moral violation. They can be precipitated by the act of a partner, friend, boss, or family member—or a stranger. They can result from facing retirement without intimacy or being in a relationship that lacks vitality, with little stimulation from within or without.

We can never be certain what will tap our unconscious and bring about a wake-up call. Many people have come to see me after their denial exploded while they were attending a lecture or watching a film. Through the years I have found I used three major defense patterns to avoid moments of knowing in my marriage as well as other relationships.

Escape: "There's nothing going on. Don't tell anyone." "I don't see what I see."

Endure: "This is all I'm really entitled to. After all, I made a commitment." "This is what commitment really is about. Maybe I want too much." "If only I could try harder. Hang in, no matter what!"

Evade: "I know he or she or it will be different when *it* [what is longed for] happens." This is the "until-ness" syndrome—evade by endless rumination and inaction.

All three result in making decisions by default.

When I escaped, endured, and evaded, I did not allow myself to feel the dilemma I faced, and so I did not act on it. In the extreme, this is what therapists call selficide, the death of the self by standing still. My friend Dick Leider, author and business consultant, refers to this as "inner kill: the art of dying without knowing it (or showing it)." Fortunately, being stuck in selficide does not have to become a lifestyle. Instead, we can choose to face the crux. This demands that we make a decision without knowing all the repercussions in advance. These decisions are crucial choices. They often represent personal commitments to our integrity.

Most of us have not had any guidance in handling our

cruxes, our crucial choices. As a result of conducting decision-making seminars, I realized I too was often uncertain about which direction to take in my career or relationships. Lack of control and not knowing what lies ahead are primary to a crux. I had to stay with my own truth, even though the path might lead to a vast, unmapped wilderness.

At the crux, often a crisis point, we are uncertain about which direction to take. Do we trust the unknown and risk to move on in a new way, or do we turn back?

Many of us face more cruxes today because we have more choices concerning commitments. For those living blind-loyalty commitments born out of role expectations, choice is seldom, if ever, factored in.

For instance, Mary, a florist, thought her marriage to Paul, a well-liked forty-six-year-old sales manager, was as solid as any she had seen. They led an active, community-involved life together and had two adolescent children. Then, after nineteen years of marriage, Paul began drinking and refused to get help. Mary faced a crucial choice. She decided to hang in, hoping and praying he would get help for recovery. She attended Al-Anon for several years and enjoyed her group's support, but her marriage became increasingly lonely. Paul still refused to go for help. One night he came home in a drunken rage and beat Mary. This was her crux: She could remain in her marriage, subjecting herself and her children to Paul's violent outbursts, or she could risk being alone and financially burdened at age forty-five.

Mary listened to her inner wisdom. She decided to down-climb—to leave her marriage. She realized that this decision was a failure only in some people's eyes. She knew that it was truly one of the wisest decisions she had made for herself in her adult life. Paul was no longer the husband she had promised to love unconditionally so many years ago. Mary found a part of herself she had never known. She knew she could no longer deceive herself. Paul had violated more than her physical body. She had found a boundary in herself she had never experienced. Now that the children were older, she was ready to risk. The context for her commitment had totally changed.

Mary felt stuck because she lacked a way to *think* about how to make decisions. She felt guilty about breaking a commitment. I told her that our realities can change dramatically. Her marriage was without meaning in the context of what had been, and what she felt would never be. Commitments end when they are without meaning.

Many of us have been unknowingly caught in a triangle called the "intrafamily marriage." I believe a high percentage of endings to relationships are attempts to unhook from this triangle—to "divorce" our parents or siblings. "Divorcing" means severing the emotional bond that binds us. A crux often involves freeing ourselves from our bond with a parent or sibling so that we can engage in adult relationships. I often suggest to people who ask, "How do you know whether to get out . . . or stay in?" that they look back at their family of origin. This was the challenge for Ric and Manuelita as they faced a crux.

Ric, a thirty-three-year-old successful electrician, was stewing over his marriage to Manuelita, a thirty-two-year-old travel agent. He said he thought their marriage was disintegrating and could no longer stand the distance between himself and his wife. He wanted Manuelita to "come in" to their marriage instead of taking trips with women friends and having an active social life that did not include him. As Ric pushed, I saw fear on Manuelita's face. She became so stiff, it was as though paralysis had set in. I asked her where she had known that feeling before. As she disclosed her story of feeling alone in her family of origin, we heard tales of her brother's physical and emotional abuse toward her. Neither parent had ever intervened; he was the "favorite." She said, "Well, intervening would not have been my father."

Manuelita eventually stated that her father was a weak

person; she was aware that at some level they all protected him. And no, she had never dealt with her anger and hurt toward men. She had never realized that she had projected her own anger and defensiveness onto Ric. She never realized that what she attributed to Ric was really her own anger of rejection.

As a child, Manuelita had protected her father's unexpressed pain and, along with her other brother, had blamed their mother. I reminded her, "The degree to which you blame is the degree to which you are stuck in your family of origin." At no time while growing up had she considered that perhaps her father was the problem, since he never took a stand with her abusive brother on her behalf and left the disciplining to his wife.

Inability to make a clean break from the family of origin also plays a major role in the most common type of divorce today: what has been called the "starter marriage." Today many young couples divorce within a few years of their wedding day. The *New York Times* described such marriages as: "brief, early marriages that end in divorce by age thirty, with no children and little more joint property than wedding gifts and a stereo. The temporary stay in marriage is much like the starter home of a generation ago, shed as the family outgrew it."

The divorce rate among couples in the 25- to 29-year age group increased fivefold from 1962 to 1992—despite the fact that this same age group did not even double in numbers during that 30-year period! While the statistics might suggest that divorce is now viewed as nothing more than a change in wardrobe, in my practice I see young people who are devastated by the ending of their brief marriages.

According to anthropologist Helen Fisher, author of *The Anatomy of Love*, divorce rates peak around the fourth year of marriage in most of the sixty-two cultures she studied. As early as the 1960s, anthropologist Margaret Mead recommended that starter marriages be called "trial" marriages. These would then become "permanent" marriages should couples decide to commit to having children. While divorce statistics do reflect our society's growing acceptance of choice, choice alone may have little to do with ethics. Yet many of our choices involve ethical challenges.

I have wondered if lack of meaning is why we see so many "starter marriages" fail. Perhaps their divorce is their first crux.

Leaving and Grieving—The Crux of It All

Grieving is essential to growth. Several aspects of leaving and grieving often are overlooked: "leaver's guilt," self-forgiveness, and saying good-bye to the dream.

Leaver's Guilt

Those of us who have decided to leave marriages and intimate relationships typically carry guilt—despite whatever led up to our leaving.

After wrestling at the crux with her decision about divorcing Matt, a forty-five-year-old printer, Julia, a forty-year-old science teacher, finally left a very troubled marriage. She realized that he was truly committed to his business and said he did not intend to change. Furthermore, he had just bought a home in another state and came home to his wife and son only every other weekend.

Julia felt great relief at making this decision, but her new choice of housing reflected her guilt. She had rented a basement apartment with dingy, worn furniture and very little light. When we talked about why she would do this when she had never in her life lived in such a place and could well afford better, Julia admitted she felt too guilty to seek more.

Self-Forgiveness

Her "lesser" living served as a self-inflicted punishment for acting on her own behalf. Julia faced a major task—to forgive herself.

One day long after her divorce, I asked Julia a question someone had asked me: "Haven't you forgiven yourself yet?" She was shocked; the idea had never entered her mind. For those who have initiated divorce in a family with children, guilt often lingers because of the pain we have caused our children—despite all our solid reasons for leaving. Hopefully we can eventually forgive ourselves and others for all that led to our decision to leave.

Saying Good-bye to the Dream

Julia thought she and Matt had reached a point of resolve when they divorced. Yet something lingered long after she had said good-bye to the commitment. She realized that his first wife had also left him for the same reasons, and she had become involved with him when he was still married. Now she wondered if the same pattern was being repeated.

When Julia was well into her therapy and focusing on letting go of the past, I asked her one day whether she had ever said good-bye to the shared dream that she and her ex-husband once had. She burst into tears, exclaiming, "That's it! No one ever named it before!" Through tears and heavy sobbing, Julia began the deep grieving of the loss of her dream.

Somewhere in the middle of my therapy with Julia, I discovered a lingering pocket of my own grief. At lunch one day my friend Ann had described the technique she had learned in a seminar on saying good-bye to the dream that couples had together. As I walked back to my office, I thought about her words. Tears ran down my cheeks. How could this be? I had been divorced for twenty years! I felt much better as I talked aloud with myself about the loss of a dream that had vanished so long ago.

Crux: A Question of Ethics

Besides divorce, there are many areas in which crucial choices need to be faced, and perhaps the most important of these are ethical challenges. Choosing what is right can free the spirit and open up our lives for further commitments. The most striking example among my clients concerned a challenge that literally meant life or death.

Today, Phyllis Pilgrim is the midlife, high-spirited fitness director of Rancho LaPuerta in Tecate, Mexico. In 1941, five-year-old Phyllis was living on Java with her American mother, her two-year-old brother, and her father, a Scotsman who was doing oil business in Java when the Japanese invaded the island. Phyllis's mother refused to take refuge in the air-raid shelter when they were told to go underground. Instead, she took her family to a hotel, where they hid under a bed. As it turned out, the bunker was totally demolished.

Phyllis's father desperately tried to move his family to Australia. However, he soon discovered that all ships commissioned to leave Java took men only. When he inquired about passage for his family, only *he* was given permission to leave.

Phyllis's father faced a crux. If he left, he could be free to provide for his family's well-being. At the same time, he knew he would be abandoning them. If he remained, there was no way of knowing how soon any of them might get out. A colleague of his did go, leaving his family behind. Phyllis's father chose to stay.

The family moved inland and kept moving up the mountain, living in one vacated house after another. They stayed clear of the Japanese for another three months. Phyllis recalls clapping her hands when she saw Japanese planes crash. The Japanese invasion continued.

In March 1942, the Japanese military took her father away. As he was forced into a truck, Phyllis and her brother and mother did not know whether they would ever see him again. Phyllis's mother managed to take care of her children by trading her personal belongings for food. Then, three weeks later, the Japanese came to take Phyllis and her brother and mother to a POW camp.

None of them knew whether the father was dead or alive until he walked into their camp at the end of the war three and a half years later. Phyllis then learned that the ship her father would have taken to Australia had been bombed. Her father's colleague, one of the ship's few survivors, had returned badly burned and been placed in the POW camp. To this day, Phyllis is still unraveling what she learned from those experiences in her formative years. She said she always appreciated her father's commitment to his family and fairness.

Of course, in the everyday world the critical choices we make are less stirring, but they are vital nonetheless. When we allow ourselves to be burdened by a system we feel is wrong, or even if we look the other way, our spirit can become tainted. And the longer we suffer, the more our ability to stand up and make a choice becomes weakened.

John, an ophthalmologist in his late thirties, was a junior partner in a successful East Coast clinic. He had been among the most successful of his medical school class. He learned that his senior partners had made a decision to lower the criteria for a particular surgical procedure to increase revenues. As a result, hundreds of trusting elderly patients would undergo unnecessary surgery.

John whispered, as though he were revealing a dark family secret, when he described his associates' pride in solving their revenue problems. Not only was this policy tricky from a legal perspective, it was also unpalatable from a medical-ethics perspective.

John grimaced as he struggled with his moral dilemma. He knew that he had to act; his conscience had spoken. He admitted it was difficult because of the rich life he had been handed by this prestigious old practice: the luxury of a fine suburban home, no financial worries, and a good savings account. John also realized that in leaving he would be saying good-bye to a high-profile circle of younger physicians.

John, facing his deep disappointment and indignation, knew that continued silence would be collusion. He said he truly felt betrayed; he had thought all his partners shared the practice's mission-statement value of integrity in service. He realized that he had to say good-bye to his commitment. And he did.

John and his family survived quite well despite the perceived risks. His story is not unlike the other business greed stories we read or hear about daily. John's choice was conscious, intentional. Not everyone's is.

Often we face a crux because of unconscious choices we made in the past. Making decisions at the time of the crux requires our making conscious choices lest we find ourselves in that same place in the future.

Some years ago I was invited to a gathering of professional colleagues to discuss First Amendment issues in relation to sex education. Several of us were on the medical school faculty, and others were clergy known for their work in the field of human sexuality. The gathering began with an elegant dinner paid for by Jeremy, a mid-sixties, weather-faced professional in the field of human sexuality.

He had summoned us to join him in defending the use of sexually explicit educational materials by testifying in various court cases around the country. He admitted that he needed people who understood the relevance of the First Amendment and had the appropriate credentials to be credible in court. All of us enthusiastically affirmed that this was our responsibility. Jeremy said we would be flying to various cities and would be highly paid for our testimony. We were delighted about the high pay, since our university faculty salaries were quite low. Our enthusiasm grew as we committed to take a stand for sex education.

Suddenly something tugged at my insides. I began to ask myself questions. "What is the subject of our testimony? And who is paying us to testify?" As my questions bubbled forth, I looked down at the coffee table and spied a videotape. Puzzled by the cover, I read the jacket. It was kiddy porn! I froze. Haltingly I searched the faces of the others around me. Had they seen the video lying there? My heart sank. Then, slowly, I asked, "Could you tell me who is backing this financially?" Jeremy replied, "Oh, some lawyers out West!" Still stunned, I made excuses and left rapidly. A good friend of mine also left immediately; he felt as troubled as I did. As I shared my concerns, he replied, "Marilyn, there is evil in the world, you know!" As soon as I arrived home, I took a long shower, wanting to wash away the creeping evil I had felt at the gathering.

I was in disbelief for days; people I knew and trusted were not questioning. The part of me who likes to be liked was challenged. I wasn't sure how to handle this crux and was concerned about the consequences, both professional and personal. I decided the issue was not debatable; I left the "project," as did my friend. I later discovered that funding was coming through lawyers who represented two notorious pornography distributors in my city.

As we learn more about facing our crux points, we learn to find our voices more readily. In contrast to the story with Jeremy, in which I left with few words, I can also remember a dramatic contrast of another crux point in which I spoke from the other end of the continuum.

Some medical school colleagues and I met in the home of one of our group to develop our climbing programs and our emerging business. I expressed my concern about safety in our outdoor programs. I suggested that we could use the professional climbing staff from Outward Bound who were in our state to ensure that we provided adequate safety backups. One of the physicians in the group said, in a haughty, arrogant tone, "No worry! We can do it. We'll use the medical model: See one, do one, teach one!"

Suddenly an angry voice erupted—it was like a roar from deep within me. "F—you! We cannot do that! We're talking about people's lives. Your training is in medicine—not rock climbing. Only one of us has had enough experience. And we had a near accident just last week when we didn't know how to get that heavy man up the rock face." All eyes were focused on me. Humiliation and deep embarrassment flooded me. To make matters worse, our host's wife had just entered the room as my expletive burst forth. I was shocked by my behavior, my total lack of control. My anger, uncensored by judgment or analysis, had a life of its own.

Only one other person in the room that night supported my perspective. I felt totally alone. It was as if a bright vision had just crashed down. This scene led to a painful crux for me; now what would I do? I needed these people—or so I thought. I left that night fully aware that I had a decision to make.

My outburst signaled the ending of my commitment to the fledgling business venture and the beginning of a down-climb. My decision to leave the group clearly was an ethical decision. My anger was indignation at my partners' lack of caring. I know now that great disappointment lay beneath my anger. Sad and angry feelings often accompany a down-climb. Mine led to my forming another company: Journeys Inward. This incident strengthened me. I now know that the down-climb after facing the crux was essential to my own growth and to my self-trust.

Restructuring a Relationship

There are many times when we choose not to end a commitment but rather to end its present form and communication dynamics and design a new contract. The crux, with its crucial choices, often reveals another route, one toward restructuring the relationship. Take this case, for instance.

Dan, a fifty-five-year-old theater director with steel-gray hair, was torn. He was leaving town on a tour, and he knew he would be visiting the city where his former drama coach and now friend lived. He felt tense about seeing Jack; he knew he had to confront him. Jack, who had been slightly drunk when they had last been together, had made a pass at Dan's wife, Kay. Dan had felt frozen in silent shame and left the scene as quickly as possible. Later he and Kay had worked through their feelings about the event.

Dan now faced a crux, which involved a commitment to his own integrity. He had two options: He could fade out of Jack's life with no further comment, or he could have an honest discussion about what had happened. If he chose the latter option, Dan realized he would have to make a final decision about his friendship depending on Jack's response. Dan felt anxious, curious, and at the same time strong.

Dan did confront the issue with Jack; his anger and pain about the betrayal poured forth. Jack listened and felt deep remorse. Jack said he felt envious of Dan's success and didn't know what to do about his envy. He admitted that his transgression with Kay had been for this reason. Jack asked Dan for forgiveness and confessed that his failure to apologize to either of them had nagged at him.

Dan was able to forgive Jack, knowing that Jack would have his own talk with Kay. This act was the initial step in restructuring their relationship. Until Dan spoke up, his integrity had been on the line. Now, as a result of their reconnecting, they could begin the rebuilding process. Dan and Jack were able to restructure their relationship into a more equal one. Jack made amends to Kay in Dan's presence, and she too forgave him. Jack and Kay were able in their fullest maturity to understand and forgive. They were able in time to see how they had grown during this episode in their marriage.

Facing a Crux Brings Growth

Facing a crux pushes us to see clearly, to become more truthful, to face humility and uncertainty, to develop conscious decision making. It challenges our integrity and pushes us to face our edges by taking risks. Commitments that allow for growth indeed have cruxes.

When I returned to Devil's Tower and faced my cruxes, I renewed my hope. Joe and Will both accommodated me so that I could have a fresh start. More important, I also renewed my contract with my self. As I climbed, something inside me changed. I had not planned it. Somehow the entire second climb felt easier than the first, and I realize now how this was another chapter in my story of my commitment to myself.

If we live a life in which we make and sustain active commitments, we will continue to encounter cruxes as we climb. A new adventure awaits us after we have acted at each crux.

Chapter 7

Beyond the Crux: Transform or Down-climb?

We shall not cease from exploration and the end of all our exploration will be to arrive where we started, and know the place for the first time.　　　—T. S. Eliot

MT. TAI SHAN, CHINA. *Late Evening. Even the incense smells ancient in this thousand-year-old Buddhist monastery. It is now called Summit Guest House, but its rooms still reflect the past. Antique silk quilts with hand-embroidered casings cover the beds. At the foot of each bed is a full-length wool fur-collared "comrade coat," or "great coat," for us to wear at dawn to watch the sun rise on Tai Shan. Night has fallen now; the only "stars" are the twinkling lights from the city below. The monastery's rule of silence—from 7:00 p.m. to 7:00 a.m.—supports our stillness. The sacred mountain invites reflection; we feel it. We found ourselves humming and singing old hymns, religious folk songs, and even Christmas carols.*

Nagging thoughts about Bob, our group member who stayed down at the base of the mountain, interrupt my stillness. We had expected an easy day today. After a fifty-mile bike ride yesterday, we were ready for an easier day. We began the morning gently doing tai chi with Luo Yao Ming, our bike guide.

We had reached Jinang Province a little later than planned. Jinang is the home of the ancient Tai Shan Temple, built between 206 B.C. and A.D. 220. After we saw this wondrous temple, we faced a series of decisions. First, the police stopped us, reporting that

a bus had slid off the mountain yesterday, killing several people. We insisted that since our group would be walking up, they need not worry about us. They finally waved us on, and we reached our destination.

The entrance path to Mt. Tai Shan was striking in its beauty. Worn, shiny ancient stones form a pathway that leads up to aged stairs worn smooth by those who have made their pilgrimages to the top. I wondered what these steep stairs, with their shallow footholds for small feet, would be like in the rain. I was relieved that we had left our luggage back at QuFu and carried light packs.

A wail abruptly interrupted my private thoughts. Cynthia, a tall, slender investment broker in her forties, had fallen on the slippery stone. She burst into tears and said she couldn't go on. She was worried that with her size-eleven shoes, she might slip again on the wet stairs. She cried in discouragement.

Yesterday, she had fallen from her bicycle and was bruised and emotionally shaken. She was especially frightened because she had fallen on her "new" knee, the one that had undergone surgery just four months earlier. The doctors had told her that she could not kneel. Friendly Chinese passersby had rushed to tend to her scrapes with fresh aloe leaves. Her fall had resulted in a decision for her. She decided to resume biking.

Today Cynthia once again was uncertain—unsure about whether to climb Mt. Tai Shan. At first she said she was afraid of what might happen to her knee while climbing up on the wet stairs. Then, through tears, she said she had also had taken some funding for her trip from a group to whom she promised a Tai Shan lecture series on her return. Weeping in dismay, she admitted, "I did not sign on for China; I was coming to climb Tai Shan. And now I have to go home and say I failed."

I asked her what the basis for her decision was. Had she examined her options? Probing deeper, I asked Cynthia what meaning she attributed to the falls. I asked why it mattered so much—not from her obligation to friends, but the inner answer. "I feel ashamed, humiliated," she blurted out. "After all, I'm supposed to do everything right; I'm not supposed to be the one to fall." We talked about her secreted false pride and her fear—both of which were crowding out her ability to make a decision from a different place. I reminded her that I was sad to see her make any decision based on humiliation and false pride.

Others in our group had gathered around Cynthia as she spoke; they listened empathically. No one tried to dissuade her from her feelings; they accepted her where she was. I asked if she was ready to make her decision from a different place—based on an entirely new foundation of what matters to her.

Cynthia continued exploring her awareness of her perfectionism. A faint smile crossed her face as she said with an emerging confidence, "I guess if I put that negative stuff aside, I could perhaps make the decision based on my strength!" Through reconstructing her beliefs, Cynthia transformed her decision to go forth with the climb. She made her decision from a place inside herself from where she could commit to the climb. She transformed the base of her decision.

A few of us walked with her while the others hiked on ahead. Cynthia said this was a first for her—to be so vulnerable in the presence of others. Cynthia would have a successful walk up Tai Shan and was exuberant when we reached the top.

We began our mountain walk with scores of friendly Chinese who make the pilgrimage every year. We had seen no other Westerners on our pilgrim route that day. Earlier we had looked up the mountainside to see pine trees that had been planted in 1730, mountain streams, numerous pagodas, and carved rocks. Now we touched those same rocks and walked past those same ancient temples built in A.D. 220. When we passed the Temple of the Goddess, the Mother of Mt. Tai, we saw scores of pairs of pilgrims' shoes outside the entrance, most of which were the tiny shoes worn by bound-foot women.

Soon we had another surprise. At the area named Halfway Gate to Heaven we were told we would have to take the cable car up the next section because the gate at the top would be closed by the time we would arrive there on foot. There before us, in sharp contrast to *the ancient rock, hung a bright red, shiny, Japanese cable car complete with Chinese Muzak.*

At his first sight of the cable car, Bob, a muscular forester in his mid-thirties, froze. He sat down and refused to go on. He rejected any invitation to talk about his feelings. With his mouth muscles tightening, Bob faced a crux. "I had a contract to bike, hike, and climb—not to ride in cable cars!" he said, glaring. I implored him to talk about what was really going on inside him. He resisted, looking fearful and angry. The group gathered around to reason him out of his terror; their efforts proved futile. It was time to back off and respect his decision. After an awkward conversation, one of our guides took him down to a hotel at the base.

Another group member, Andy, a poet, came forth with a line from Faust: "Of suns and worlds I've nothing to be quoted, how [people] torment themselves is all I've noted." We smiled in recognition, knowing fully how each one of us had faced some "torment" because of some personal crux on this trip.

At four-thirty the next morning, a howling wind served as our alarm clock. At five, bundled in our great coats and caps, we gathered with our flashlights for the walk to Sunrise Peak. At first we seemed to be alone, but as faint light appeared, we began to see numerous figures walking alongside us. At the mountain's edge, increasing light revealed clusters of pilgrims on the surrounding rocks. I felt like I was part of a blended culture for a moment. Neither clothing nor language separated East from West here.

Suddenly, I saw the famous rock I had seen in the books, its solid mass jutting dramatically into the sky, as though thrusting itself toward another world. Chinese folklore tells us this is where the sun begins its westward journey across the sky. People covered the rocks like human moss—above us, below us, behind us, and all the way up to the temple. Then a murmur ran through the crowd; the rise in energy was palpable. Above the horizon but before the top of the haze, the first hint of red appeared. Ming whispered, "Like a baby in the womb." We all stared together. It felt like prayer. I thought of Simone Weil's statement: "Absolute unmixed attention is prayer."

As the sun continued to climb, the surrounding mountains became more distinct, breaking through the mist that enshrouded them. I thought about the meaning of the sunrise.

Perhaps reillumination is what we pursue when we seek out the beautiful sunrises in the world. And perhaps this is why we typically meet these experiences in silence. I was pondering this specialness when someone reminded me it was time to start our long descent.

The queasiness many of us had felt at the top quickly turned into wrenching diarrhea. Weary and weak, we felt relief and ease when we reached our hotel. As soon as we could, we gathered together with Bob to hear his story, which was uneventful. Bob looked relaxed, yet we could easily read his clear message: "Don't ask me." We all put the event behind us.

Beyond the Crux

Often a person's crux may seem rather trivial to others, but his or her fear are not. For Cynthia, her crucial choice had been either to risk further injury after her bike spill or to face the massive disappointment and sense of isolation she would feel if she walked away from fulfilling a deeply personal desire. Bob's crux (hypothetically) had been either to expose his vulnerability, his fear, to a group he had known for only eight days or face the shame and disconnection he would feel if he said no to the group and the experience.

A crux means being "between a rock and a hard place"—and most of us have been there. Either choice held meaningful consequences for both Cynthia and Bob. Both these situations emerged for Cynthia and Bob as insoluble problems, yet both did choose.

Cynthia was open to talking about her fears and disclosing her frustration. She was able to think out loud about her crux. She also had a highly motivating force—her personal investment in climbing Mt. Tai Shan. In his down-climb, Bob had listened to his inner voice and feelings.

While it would be easy to judge Bob's decision negatively, none of us knew what lay at the base of his fear. In fact, perhaps his saying no to the group was another "edge" in his commitment to himself.

Change—From Within

It took me some time to realize that most real and lasting changes come from dealing with unexpected life events. I grew up in an era when we truly thought we could plan our lives and the changes we made. Today I know that most changes are life interruptions, shifting us onto an irrational plane without any preparation. We have all seen people who make many changes in the hope that change itself will alter their lives.

We do not need to end every commitment at a crux by down-climbing, or leaving. Often we need to focus on the crucial choice and examine the facts, the history, and our values and limits. Some people think they need to end a relationship when they encounter a crux: a friend's betrayal, a verbally abusive boss, the news that the top position at work was given to someone you don't like, or an organization's misuse of your money. Others decide to make changes in the implicit contract by naming the behavior and asking for change and accountability. This sets the foundation for a new relationship and hopefully a better future.

Just as we don't need to climb a mountain to awaken our "within," we don't need to go somewhere else to find ourselves. Howard Thurman once said that until we are at home somewhere, we cannot be at home everywhere. I like to think that that "somewhere" lies within ourselves.

I remember a personal transformation experience. Years ago as part of my professional training, I co-led a couples therapy group. The other therapist, a professor in my department in the medical school, was using a new technique that allowed one person to use a mind-control method that I felt was disrespectful and power-based. I felt dismay not only because I disagreed with his approach but also because he was my supervisor. I needed his signature to prove I had completed the 1,500 hours of supervision required for professional licensure.

At first I tried to adapt. Then I tried to work around his highly directive approach that ran so counter to my philosophy. All the while I saw couples retreating; some did not show up for the group meetings. I spoke with friends, I lay awake. I knew I had no choice but to speak to him.

I faced a crux. I decided that no license hanging on a wall was worth forfeiting my integrity. I had to speak truthfully about what I felt and risk that he might not recommend me. As I look back, I am not certain if he was fully aware of the power he held because of his senior role. Then I automatically gave him even more power through my silence, fear, and accommodation! But at the time it did not matter. I made an appointment to meet with him. I was fully prepared to walk away.

With tears streaming down my face in frustration and indignation, I blurted out all my concerns about his approach. "That is way too much control over clients, and you don't even know their history. And you are treating people like they are objects—things to be done to. Furthermore, I feel shameful about my silence, and no matter what, you need to know that no license is worth this betrayal of my integrity."

To my surprise, he listened to me. He said he would examine his behavior and said how much he respected me for standing up to him. I felt relief; he was, after all, the fine person I had known him to be. As a result, we were able to negotiate an entirely new cooperative work contract in which our roles were equal and we used a combination of approaches, including clients' perspectives about their needs in our work. By facing this crux head-on, I was able to open the door to the possibility for change.

Transformation can be even more far-reaching, to the point that a person decides to change course entirely. No matter how doggedly we pursue our careers, we have to be alive to that sudden wake-up call. For someone I know, this came from the most unlikely source: a dream.

Chuck has been steadily climbing the ladder in the advertising world. He had begun as a mail clerk, then moved up to copywriter, and eventually became an account executive, handling a large sporting-goods account. He was doing well economically, but felt tired and empty much of the time due to high-stress deadlines. Chuck was single, yet hardly had time for either men or women friends with the high demands of his work. One night Chuck and his friends talked about their visions. He talked about his true passion— writing short stories. Since his promotion in advertising, he'd had little time for his writing. He made a commitment to take some steps toward fulfilling his vision.

That night he had a dream in which he saw himself sitting in a cage, with a book on a nearby shelf. He awakened with sadness and decided it was time to make a change. The money was simply not worth his forfeiture of his passion. He went into his senior vice-president's office and told him about his decision to make time for his writing. Chuck realized there was a strong likelihood that they would let him go. He asked if he could work part-time as a copywriter and turn his account executive position over to one of the other senior copywriters who longed for the position. Fortunately, Chuck's boss agreed. He told him he would agree to that rather than lose him. Chuck was able to transform his work to move toward his vision. Today Chuck has published several short stories and spends far more hours at his writing than he ever did as an account executive.

Changing the basis of long-term relationships can be the hardest challenge of all. Family links, either between a parent and child or between spouses, become so steeped in habit that they might as well as forged in steel. Breaking free of these chains is vital to transformation, however, and is often the only way the relationship can gain new life.

Jane, a mid-fifties human relations professor who had a reputation for her involvement in human rights causes, came in to recount the story of her visit home to see her dying father. She reported that she had reached her father's bedside while he was still alive. Joining her was her authoritarian mother. Jane's sobs deepened as she thrust her brightly painted fingernails before me. "As I stood at my dad's bedside, my mother ordered me to go downstairs to the beauty shop in the hospital and get a manicure. And, never questioning, I did! But when I returned, my father was dead." Jane, who had been very close to her father, was astonished by her blind obedience to her mother, who, while sweet in public, was domineering at home. In a whispered tone of astonishment, she continued, "And I had never in my life had a manicure."

Jane added, "Well, I'm through with my mother. I will never forgive her for this. I am just not going to see her anymore. Besides, I cannot tolerate her constant criticism and her interference with my two daughters."

I reminded her that part of this decision stemmed from her grief. She was angry—with herself as well as with her mother. I reminded her that she owed it to herself, and her children, to speak out and see what came of it. "In addition," I reminded her, "you will never truly be free if you make a cutoff of this kind—your mother matters too much to you."

As Jane recounted the scene with her mother, she realized she had felt like an eleven-year-old girl when she had automatically obeyed her mother's order. This jolted her into an awareness of how her childhood pattern of giving her power to her mother was alive and well at an unconscious level. Jane poured out many stories interlaced with deeply buried feelings about feeding her mother's self-image and self-worth over the years.

Jane's unfinished business from her childhood later became a crux. Her moment of knowing revealed a delayed consequence of unconscious loyalty, described in Chapter 6. As a result of this initial awareness, with its nail polish reminder, she began to explore her family history and her fusion with her mother that had bound her in such unknown ways. In the midst of this she also realized that when her mother had sent her down for a manicure, she was unconsciously attempting to protect her from pain.

Jane was soon able to move beyond her childhood loyalty with its no-choice reaction and create an adult loyalty, one with an honest voice. In time, Jane not only used her adult voice with her mother but also realized there was no need for her to cut herself off. She did, of course, let her mother know what she had needed from her as a child and began standing up to her. The mother-daughter hostility gradually shifted into a much more equal *adult* mother to *adult* daughter relationship. Jane and her mother eventually transformed their relationship. As Jane looked back, she was able to feel gratitude for the growth, the "gift in the crisis."

One of the most common cruxes I have seen involves couples facing possible divorce. Three prevailing attitudes of couples help shape the decision at the marriage crux and affect the changing ethos of marital commitment.

"I think my parents died of marriage."

Steven's parents' marriage reflected a passive, static commitment based on duty and obligation. Commitment to them meant loyalty and longevity—"till death do us part." According to Webster's dictionary, the word *commit* means "to obligate one's self, to pledge" or "to put into a place to be kept safe." Steven's parents literally did just that. They had committed themselves to the institution of marriage.

Their marriage was an amalgam of boredom, suffering, and grim duty, which both admitted in their own way to Steven.

"I have not had failed marriages; I have been married three different times—each at a different stage in my development."

Margaret Meade never expressed any guilt about her three marriages. Her attitude was one grounded on a developmental model. The quote above was her response when she was asked about the "failed" marriages. She concluded that she had made a good marital choice at each different developmental stage in her life. She obviously realized she carried these relationships in her and they would remain forever. Her perspective is often spoken about today since we are living such long lives.

"I have been 'married' seven times—each time to the same man and without divorce."

Pat and Ken's marriage reflected an active, alive, growth-centered commitment nurtured by free choice. Both had learned how to give themselves in commitment, reflecting the part of the root definition, *mitterre*, to "send" their word into another. Pat and Ken seemed to know that they, like most of us, will never see the grand rewards of commitment touted in films and novels. "Divorce was never an option," they said as they quietly committed to making changes that would accommodate each other's personal growth and transform their marriage. Pat joined Ken's groups interested in alternative medicine, and Ken joined Pat's book and lecture group.

As these attitudes reflect, there is no single attitude toward marriage today. Key to our own value about marriage is our ability to continue to be aware and to reexamine who and how we are in our relationships—to understand transformations.

Bud, a distinguished mid-fifties management director, had participated in a training program called the Fundamentals of Rapid Change at his company's request and expense. Bud's background was in mechanical engineering, and he had had little training in developing what we refer to now as E.Q., his emotional quotient or feeling expressiveness. This training program had resulted in remarkable changes in Bud's awareness both personally and in his communication with others. He learned to identify his feelings, to share them with others, to give and receive feedback while carefully listening. He learned how to relax and look someone in the eyes when he spoke. He learned how to respect differences and became more honest about himself.

He made dramatic changes at work, and his wife, Muriel, a sensitive, supporting homemaker, began to notice and delight in his changes at home. He began to listen more attentively to her and no longer hid behind the newspaper. He began to grieve his pending retirement.

Bud was so intrigued with the differences that Rapid Change was making in his own and others' lives that he decided to become a part of the organization after his early retirement. As he thought about working at home and being with his wife of thirty-five years on a full-time basis, he began to stew. He realized he would be giving up the esteem, respect, and other emotional support he received at the office. He contrasted this with being home alone in an unsatisfying marriage.

Bud decided that he had to talk with Muriel. He had looked at various relatives' and some friends' marriages, and knew he wanted something more than just complacent existence. He was willing to separate and possibly divorce rather than live in an empty marriage. Bud truly faced a crux, and decided he had to speak out.

Bud spoke with Muriel one evening and was honest about his old, buried feelings about their relationship. They both believed their marriage had been "without love for the past twelve years." Muriel was not surprised but was disappointed that she might not share in the "new" Bud as father, husband, and grandfather. Both went to bed in pain.

When they awoke the next morning, Muriel began to share her pain and anger that had accumulated over the years as they had slowly drawn apart. They talked almost nonstop for three days. They brought up old wounds, buried hurts, and anger. They began to let each other know who they truly were. They cried, they remembered, they disclosed deep emotions and feelings that they had never before divulged.

Both spoke sincerely and with respect for the other's feelings. They began to look forward to talking together. Almost daily conversations have continued. They said they have talked more than they had in the last twenty years—if not the entire marriage! They both changed themselves so much that there was constantly something new to be discovered in each other.

Muriel and Bud made the decision to recommit to a new understanding of their marriage vows and to their family. They continue to have an ongoing series of discussions about their past, their present, and expectations for the future. They took the opportunity to tell their adult children one by one what was happening and tell them the story of their marriage.

One day Bud remarked to me, "I think I'm falling in love all over again with my wife!" It was not long before the two decided to have a recommitment ceremony over a Thanksgiving weekend. Their children and their spouses and their five grandchildren gathered for the special occasion. Bud and Muriel wrote a beautiful, touching "Reflections on Marriage," which they and their children read together at the service. An excerpt reads: "We know that not all marriages are meant to be; however, the goal should be for life, and all avenues of respectful communication must be open along with the desire to make it work." Bud and Muriel are committed to this pledge. Mature, compassionate, and trusting, they can live with the foundation: "In matters of the heart, I love you and I trust you are two stepping-stones across the stream."

As I think about Muriel and Bud, I am impressed by how much we can change if we tell the truth. They did all this without therapy! They continue to keep their marriage alive with their new commitment to each other and to their transformed marriage.

The Driving Force: Caring

Many of us who have looked back on the remarkable changes in our relationships have asked the question: "What drove these changes?" I believe it is our genuine deep caring. When we truly commit from this depth, we begin to transform all our commitments. The range of sacrifice is on a continuum from small to great.

Recently, Yiga, a twenty-six-year-old Tibetan woman, joined five other Tibetans in a hunger strike that took place near the United Nations building in New York. These six Tibetans were willing to die to make the cause of Tibetan freedom heard by the United Nations on its fiftieth anniversary. At a time when American government and business leaders are working to increase trade with China, the fasters wanted to remind them and the rest of the world about China's occupation of Tibet. They wanted the U.N. to intervene, to set up talks with the Tibetans in exile. Yiga had vowed to die before she would abandon her protest.

She weakened early in her fasting, yet refused to eat. The Dalai Lama personally intervened and asked the group to leave the site and change their strategy. Yiga, in her semi-conscious state, was hospitalized for intravenous feeding. After returning to Minneapolis, Yiga transformed her method but not her commitment. She still speaks for others "who have no voice."

Yiga's story forces us to ask the ultimate commitment question: "What or whom are we willing to die for?" Yiga's actions may not have influenced U.S. government policy toward China or ignited world opinion, but at least Tibet's plight has been discussed once again at the U.N. The remarkable point is that an immigrant, a yak-herder's daughter from the high Himalayas who speaks little English, gained the attention of the secretary general of the United Nations.

Acts such as Yiga's remind me that each commitment is an action that contributes to the whole. Consciousness changes slowly. Yiga's story challenges us to look deep into ourselves, into the possibilities for transformation, connecting the personal and the political with the whole. Yiga's inner climb to a goal she believes to be sacred reminds me of our personal journeys into the spirit in commitment.

Chapter 8

Bedrock: The Core of Commitment and Caring

Until one is committed, there is hesitancy, the chance to draw back, always ineffectiveness. . . . The moment one definitely commits oneself, then Providence moves.

—Goethe

MT. EVEREST BASE CAMP. *We are finally here! Today was staggering. This afternoon we finally approached Pang-La Pass at 17,000 feet. I gasped when I saw the full range of white mountains against a bright blue sky. Four of the highest snowy peaks in Tibet—including Mt. Everest—stood in massive display before us. In blustering winds, waves of wonder steadied us in silence and sacred awe as we stood before these imposing timeless giants.*

Later the winds visited our tent site. We walked around the barren area to keep warm, concentrating on our breathing, which was difficult at this high altitude. Our guides set up tents in the ragged gales. We were surprised when we saw them trying to stake down a four-sided canvas "toilet tent" in the frozen ground. Within minutes it pulled itself up and danced out of sight across the plateau!

After we settled in with our packs, we began our hike slowly toward Camp One over glacial debris. Breathing demanded attention, but I would not complain. The young Tibetan woman who had accompanied our driver, Tenzin, was lying in the truck taking oxygen. Always aware of our pacing at this oxygen-scarce altitude, we stayed keenly present-minded as we moved purposefully over the boulders.

Brightly colored expedition tents from American, Italian, and Japanese expeditions interrupted the vista of brown-gray scree. We faced harsh winds and overwhelming geological wonder. Stones and debris from ancient sedimentary deposits were stacked up to form ridges that looked like the work of a colossus stonemason.

In a welcome relief, the sun briefly cast its glow on Mt. Everest, and Iris and I witnessed Mother Nature's most brilliant light show. I was overwhelmed that this spectacle of compressed limestone towering before us was once a part of the floor of an ancient ocean. How slowly these cataclysmic forces have shaped the Himalayan range.

As we hiked over the gigantic mounds of rock rubble, I thought about the ancient peoples who had viewed mountains as the dwelling place between heaven and earth of the spirits—gods, ghosts, monsters, and demons. Then, after the Enlightenment, as horizons of the world changed, so did points of view. These mountains, now seen as awesome, were once depicted as a horror.

We continued upward to a lovely vista that overlooked a frozen ocean pinnacled with glacial ice. Nature had painted the tips of the waves with a faint blue-green watercolor wash. We didn't linger. The nearly gale-force wind was harsh; breathing was exhausting. When we returned to our camp site, several yaks approached in their decorated headdresses. I was envious of how they appeared so sturdy in their warm winter coats.

Now back in the tent I feel the warmth of protection. My fingers are stiff from the cold. I see why Tibetans sleep snuggled in circles around the fire. Privacy is not on the list of Tibet's rich offerings. Somehow its absence reminded me that our true privacy would have to come from within.

We had come a long way since our first days in Tibet. No words or pictures could have prepared us for our visit to Jokhang Monastery and its overpowering assault on our senses. Pilgrims prostrated themselves at the old, worn monastery steps. Tenzin told us that many people come to the monastery in Lhasa now that the Chinese government had lessened its control over Tibet's religious practices. As

we entered into semidarkness, we saw towering effigies of Bod-
hisattvas, gods, and demons draped in brocade and gold threads.
Iris, Abby, and I stared at one another when Tenzin told us that
the innermost shrine contains the most precious, oldest object in
Tibet—the original statue of Sakyamuni, the historical Buddha.

As we made our way through the yellow, half-lit halls we heard
monks chanting their mantras, reciting from their ancient scriptures
as they sat in their cross-legged lotus position before the mammoth
Buddhas. Only one sign of modernity stood out: Almost every
monk had a thermos of yak-butter tea next to his scripture stand.
The strong aroma of incense blended with the pungent smell of
burning yak butter that hung heavily in the air. Pilgrims left coins
and paper money at various god and Buddha statues; some left traditional white scarves to honor the deities. Small photos or postcards
of the Dalai Lama were propped next to the burning votives. Scores
of pilgrims, engrossed in prayer with their prayer beads, murmured
mantras as they steadily wound their way through the temple pas-
sages. Some carried small pails of yak butter to replenish the lamps.
The monks blessed them as they passed through. This was our last
stop before we left Lhasa for the contrasting Tibetan Plateau.

Traveling across the Plateau was unlike any other drive I have
ever made. Tenzin stopped the vehicle at every small mountainside
shrine, with life-giving stream outlets in the rock, and bathed his
head. He would then drink a handful of water. Wanting to join
him in his ritual, we streaked the water over the top of our heads.
Fully understanding tourists' fear of mountain dysentery, Tenzin
politely ignored our not joining him in drinking the water. I welcomed these shrine stops—not only for the ritual but also because
they interrupted the terror we felt while driving over the shoulderless,
rough road with its sheer thousand-foot drops.

As we neared the Mt. Everest region, we began to encounter
nomadic life. Unlike the dung-covered houses in small villages or the
white-washed stone houses around Lhasa, the nomads live in felt
tents made of moistened yak hair that is beaten and squeezed until
it forms a felt layer. I am struck with the simplicity of their lives and

*their close connection to their natural world as they move with their
cattle while herding them into the "warmer" climate.*

*I sense what D. H. Lawrence wrote when he said: "Different
places on the face of the Earth have different vital effluence, different
vibration, different chemical exhalation, different polarity with different stars; call it what you like. But the spirit of place is a great
reality."*

*Here in Tibet I can feel this sense of connection to the universe.
Each upheaval in our lives reshapes us; we are alive as the mountain
is alive. I am so fully aware here of who I am in the world—a tiny
speck connected to all life. The Himalayas speak to me of human
nature. Just as with humans, what we see of the mountains are
merely the visible uppermost tips of their deep underlying structures
shaped by nature's forces. I thought about my own neglect of the
spiritual, the invisible.*

Back to the Invisible

One star-filled night during a safari Thad and I led in
Tanzania, East Africa, we gathered around the fire at the
ridge above Empaki Crater. Our Maasai guides had joined us
in what had become a ritualized evening circle. Robert Bly
told a lovely story that night, an African story that Thad
translated to our Maasai guides and donkey men.

*Once upon a time there was a man who had twelve cows,
and he loved his cows. Every morning and evening he would
praise them for the amount of milk they were giving and for
their beauty. One morning he noticed that the amount of milk
had lessened. Each day for a week he noticed the same thing.
So that night he decided to stay up and see what was going on.*

*About midnight, he happened to look up at the stars, and
he saw one star that seemed to be getting larger. It was—and
the light got stronger as the star came closer and closer to earth.*

It came straight down toward his cow pasture and stopped a few feet from him in the form of a great ball of light. Inside the light was a luminous woman. As soon as her toes touched the ground, the light disappeared and she became an ordinary woman.

He asked her, "Are you the one who has been stealing milk from my cows?"

"Yes," she said, "my sisters and I like the milk from your cows very much."

He said, "You are very beautiful. And I'm glad that you like my cows. And so this is what I want to say: If you marry me, we can live together, and I will never hit you and you won't have to take care of the cows all the time. I'll take care of them part of the time myself. Will you marry me?"

She responded slowly, "Yes, I will. But there's one condition. I have brought this basket with me, and I want you to agree that you will never look into this basket. You must never look into it, no matter how long we are married. Do you agree to that?"

"Oh, I do," he said.

So they were married, and they lived together very well for six or seven months. Then one day, while she was out herding the cows, he happened to notice the basket in a corner of the house. He said to himself, "Well, you know, she is my wife, so it could be considered my basket!" After he had said this, he opened the basket and then began to laugh. "There's nothing in the basket! There's nothing in the basket! There's absolutely nothing in the basket! Nothing! There's nothing in the basket!" He kept saying these words and laughed so loudly that his wife eventually heard his laughter.

She came into the hut and asked him, "Have you opened the basket?"

He began laughing again. "I did!" he said. "I opened the basket! There's nothing in it! There's nothing in the basket at all! There's absolutely nothing in the basket! Nothing is in the basket!"

She said, "I have to leave now. I have to go back."
He cried out, "Don't go! Don't leave me!"
She said, "I have to go back now. What I brought with
me in the basket was spirit. How like you humans to think
there is nothing where there is spirit."
And she was gone.

This ending in the story reminded me of how often I have thought there was nothing where there was spirit. I have often distanced myself from respect for the invisible, the mystery. At times absorbed in my material life as fully as the Tibetans are in their religious practices, I can easily be lulled into spiritual flatness.

This results in a dulled soul, a condition visible in the glazed eyes that reflect the ravages of loneliness, discouragement, depression, cynicism, and isolation. Spiritual flatness shows itself in lack of vitality. Too often I see people who believe they do not matter to anyone.

Often I wonder what role conspicuous consumption plays in the deadening of the spirit. Thomas Wolfe said, "American businessmen don't pray; they support the arts." Are we spiritually flat because of our consumerism, greed, and capitalism, or are we driven to consumption because of our spiritual flatness? One could argue for both, but I truly believe that we can live in a consumer culture and still be spiritually alive, despite society's betrayals.

Betrayals

Many Americans have traditionally turned to religion for their spirituality. I hear many client stories of folks no longer trusting religious institutions. They feel betrayed—not by their religious doctrines, but by leadership misconduct. They cite sexual and/or financial misconduct of the likes of Tammy Faye and Jim Bakker and Jimmy Swaggart, each a trusted, self-proclaimed guardian of the spirit. Many who seek to integrate religion and spirituality move cautiously, knowing fully of the tyranny of some religious commitments that entice the vulnerable.

Exposés of gullible people who give themselves over to a cult movement abound. As I consulted with troubled church groups, I found one common thread: The powers of patriarchy protected the secrets. Obviously, such betrayal has not been limited to Protestant religions. I have consulted with Jewish groups that faced moral and ethical struggles in their synagogues. By the end of 1988, the Catholic church had been forced to pay $19 million to families of children abused by priests. Nor do the Eastern religions fare much better. According to one survey, thirty-four of fifty-four gurus had had sex with one or more of their students. The good news is that religious communities are now taking the lead in seeking help to self-regulate adherence to their ethical guidelines. Also, they are addressing the fact that they have not examined the power given them as religious leaders.

When I sat on a national professional council before which professional ethics charges were heard, I saw that the highest number of charges were related to the clergy's abuses of power.

I have often told the story about a client, a recovering alcoholic incest victim who had been abused by her clergy counselor. When she finally revealed her secret, she said, "I think he tore my soul." The renewal of hope and faith can take a long time.

Many of my clients, including clergy, have buried feelings of despair and hurt. These jammed-up feelings can block energy necessary for spiritual growth. I often explain to clients that the process of healing may seem at first like using Drano, as jammed feelings—the gunk, the shame, the pain—surface. Yet only when we can name our feelings and express our pain and understand the abuse of power can we begin to heal and face our spiritual hunger.

Spiritual Hunger

Despite betrayals, Americans still have faith. Some ninety percent of Americans have never doubted the existence of God, eighty percent believe in miracles, and ninety percent pray at some time during the week. Sixty-seven percent of Americans report having psychic, mystical, or paranormal experiences. We all are witness to the fastest-growing socio-spiritual movement in America in recent years—the twelve-step programs that grew out of Alcoholics Anonymous.

Secular spirituality is no longer alien to the millions of Americans who are seeking esoteric spiritual paths. Those who have spurned patriarchal, "god-outside" religion are now searching for union with the invisible. As author-therapist Joann Krestan stated, "It doesn't matter what *it* is—as long as *you* ain't it." Witness entire sections of bookstores filled with books on ecofeminism, the corporate soul, witch-craft, the Goddess, Buddhism, Gaia, Native American spiri-tuality, and Christian mysticism, to name but a few. As in other movements, marketeers have moved in with crystals, Tarot cards, I Ching, angels, and divination cards. Even the Ouija board is back. Some wonder why the public buys mil-lions of poorly written books on spirituality. I believe it is because we long to connect with our spirituality.

Spirituality is difficult to define. I define it as: that place in us where the utterly intimate and vastly infinite meet—our connection to the universe and with all that is. It is our oneness with our higher power, nature, god or goddess. Spirituality is not necessarily religiosity; it may or may not encompass religious beliefs and/or practices.

Our spiritual pursuits illustrate our hunger for meaning and purpose. Baby boomers, labeled by some as a generation of seekers, have returned to religion, with fifty-three percent now attending a church, mosque, or synagogue. Many clients tell me about their feeling of being cut off from their ancient life connections.

A few years ago my friend Eleftheri and I led a group to northern Greece and Crete. The focus of the trip was "Passage to Partnership." Riane Eisler, author of *The Chalice and the Blade*, and UCLA professor of archeology Marija Gimbutas, whose goddess civilization research was the basis for Eisler's work, joined us as guest lecturers.

Marija led us through the ancient ruins at Sessklos, the site of her early digs and a source for her book *The Goddess Civilization*. As we stood at the Goddess site, surrounded by ancient, dry, rounded earth forms, listening attentively to Marija's stories, several women simultaneously burst into tears. Deep, quiet sobs rose in me like rolling waves from the core of my being. They were different from any tears I had ever shed. I asked myself what was going on—what was the connection here—and why I was so connected to this place. What did my sobs mean?

I soon discovered a missing cornerstone of my life story—my grief over the loss of a part of our history, the Goddess civilization, that had so long been denied us. Marija explained that in the pre-Cretan Goddess civilization, men and women were equal and lived in true partnership. Their art reflected her theories. In Sessklos we had touched a key piece of our bedrock truth. This knowledge, while painful, restored my hope for the future. After the flood of tears, I felt a deeper sense of wonder and a strong connection to the other men and women in our group. I felt their mutual caring as well.

Academic recognition and acceptance of Marija's scholarly work have come begrudgingly in the U.S. Findings that retold the Cretan history and art take time for acceptance within a culture. I believe we were meant to be in Greece at that time with Marija. I am more open than ever to synchronicity and life's surprises.

Synchronicity

What I call synchronicity today I would have called coincidence in the past. A friend recently said it differently: "God's just choosing to be anonymous again."

I met seventy-five-year-old Jacqueline Van de Putte in a spiritual community in the south of France. She was an archetype of spiritual strength to me. Jacqueline was the first woman agricultural engineer in France, an accomplishment for which her elitist family disinherited her. She also studied philosophy and had become very excited about a process known as sophrology, a meditation method used by many European physicians, healers, and athletes, including Olympic athletes who want to develop mind-body awareness. Jacqueline was centered, mature, and loving.

Some years ago I visited her in Spain, where I was conducting a workshop at a humanistic psychology conference. Jacqueline was excited when she announced that following our visit she was going to an island off the coast with Nansky, her friend of thirty-five years. Jacqueline stood next to a trunk filled with books about sophrology and philosophy and announced, "My dear, I am so excited—I am going to teach Nansky ze Method."

"But, Jacqueline," I responded, "surely after all these years you have taught Nansky some of the sophrology method!"

"No, my dear, I have not," she replied.

"But why on earth haven't you when it means so much to you?" I asked.

"My dear," she said with a pause, "she never asked until now."

Once again I had learned another valuable lesson from Jacqueline.

Some years later, I had another synchronicity experience. I had flown out to San Diego to surprise my mother on her seventy-fifth birthday. When my sister Sue met me at the airport, I told her that I wanted Mother to hold me, but that asking her felt like a risk, since only children were hugged or held.

Shortly after my surprise arrival, which thoroughly delighted my mother, I entered my niece's bedroom and sat on the bed. Suddenly my mother came up behind me and swooped me into her arms! I wept with joy. I did not have to ask. I realize this experience was more than coincidence; what I shall never know is which one of us had been holding out.

I realize my risking came from my caring. In my younger years I never realized how changing my relationships in my personal life had anything to do with action in the public, political domain. My voice became stronger; I became more active in community actions.

The Connection: Personal and Political

Personal change often cannot be separated from social and political change, even though the connection is not always distinct. As we commit to ourselves, and to others, we can create social change. By speaking out and garnering public attention, we can make a difference.

Outside Arusha, Tanzania, a group of young women left their villages to study in Nairobi. Away from their traditional villages, they learned about the effects of genital mutilation. For example, they learned that in 1982, after fourteen girls died of the tragic effects of this mutilation, the president of Kenya banned the age-old practice. (As a result of immigration, this practice is now occurring in the United States.) The young women also learned, as told in Alice Walker's book *Possessing the Secret of Joy*, that more than ninety million of the women and girls now living in Africa, the Far East, and the Middle East have been genitally mutilated in the name of tradition. Nine of ten women become "frigid," a psychological effect of circumcision.

As these young women returned to their villages and educated their mothers, the women of several African villages have put a stop to clitoridectomy. This change was very difficult, since women often perpetuate the custom and fight to keep it, believing they will be "unacceptable" if they do not submit to it. Still, a group of committed—and connected—women prevailed.

Human rights issues are global, not local issues. Creating change for human rights is a responsibility we all can act on by speaking out. Without broad public support, few of the labor laws, child welfare laws, and civil rights laws we now enjoy would not have been passed. It was only by staging a national sexual strike that the women of Iceland won the right to vote. None of these public stands for human and civil rights could have happened without community, without the power from many voices. It is often in public actions that the "invisible Americans"—invisible because of race and class—become visible.

I believe as changes slowly take place over time, we see a change in awareness, in consciousness. Spirits rise. I call this a soul shift. This most powerful change of all comes from yet another place within—from bedrock. This is the sacred realm of the ancients, God, the Goddess, Yahweh, intuition, and the unconscious. Here we find the voice of the "Wise One."

I began using the term "Wise One" in a therapy session one day with a woman named Rebecca, a highly competent lecturer and author. She had always struggled with making decisions even though she had all the factual information she could find. Slightly frustrated one day, I said, "You are using too much reason and logic; I think you need to use more of your intuition. Are you willing to try something different?" Rebecca, tired of her indecisiveness, was most willing. I asked her to close her eyes, and I used guided imagery to lead her down deep into herself—into her bedrock of knowing, her soul—where she could turn to the Wise One within for her answer. I asked her to seek the wisdom that she had within her and to trust that the response would be true for her. When I later guided her back to the present, she had a soft smile on her face. "I got my answer; I'm going to Blank Publishing, and I know it's the right decision." Throughout the remainder of Rebecca's therapy we used imagery whenever she encountered her indecisiveness.

The Wise One is our center of highest consciousness and true knowing. It is from here that we "get it," that we are awake, that we know our own truth. At bedrock, I am aware of the part of me that I commit from most truly. It is the home of the soul.

In listening to our Wise One, we develop an inner strength that draws others to us. Some wiser people have integrated this inner spiritual strength so fully that they are models for us all.

Speaking Truth to Power

We cannot speak the truth to power until we know our own truth. Knowing our truth means we must know ourselves before we can speak out. Typically, we Americans have an us-versus-them mentality when it comes to changing our institutions. We refer to "those churches," "those schools," "those political parties," and "those business practices." Yet we are our institutions. Our denial of this fact has led to social disintegration. We have turned our power over to power seekers.

Institutions are people. We cannot wait for government in Washington to change. No church can give us spirituality; no religious or secular ceremony will keep a marriage alive. And no school can ignite our desire to learn. We can move from helplessness—the result of passive reliance on control-

ling institutional structures—to active, participatory involvement to solve our problems. This active participation takes
many forms besides public actions. Some give money, some
pray or meditate, and some speak to the issues in large or
small informal groups. Each of us can make a difference.
Thus, we can redefine and reform our life commitments and
thus shape society from our deepest values.

We can speak truth to power by using our personal ethics
to make responsible choices in all our primary relationships.
I believe our caring about others' souls can ignite our
political consciousness. A friend said, "You're confusing
spirituality and politics." I replied, "No, I'm not. I am integrating spirituality and politics; they have been separated too
long. Our caring concern can make a difference."

A decade ago a group of us who called ourselves People
Against Military Madness engaged in nonviolent civil disobedience in response to defense issues, including nuclear
proliferation. We participated in a series of large actions that
resulted in many of us going to jail.

To risk arrest was one of the most relevant experiences in
my adult life. It was an excellent opportunity to stand up for
what I believed. A group of ten of us were arrested for
climbing a high chain-link fence at the Honeywell Corporation, a multibillion-dollar company that manufactures guidance systems for nuclear missiles, nuclear weapons, and
conventional military weapons. We poured our blood on
the front door to symbolize all the deaths of innocent people
dying in Asia from cluster bombs made by Honeywell.

In court, I felt a bit uncertain about appearing without an
attorney; we represented ourselves. One by one we told the
jury our stories of what had led us to civil disobedience.

Judge Isabel Gomez-Edwards made the following comments following the verdict:

> I have the task of weighing what this infraction on
> this occasion, by these defendants, means. And what I

have seen before me in this trial is a group of ten people, each of whom is fully engaged in his or her life, who cherishes his or her life and the lives around him or her on the planet; who works to empower others to achieve their own individual integrity; and who is motivated by a very hard-won personal knowledge of his or her own being. It is clear to me that the collective virtuous acts of this group far outweigh the infraction committed here. . . .

And I would like to use the authority of this court to encourage you to further recognize your own—the size and shape of your own individual—power. . . . It is not ideas—which in this case are rather commonly heard ideas—or facts, which in this case are facts which, however numbed some of us may be to their meaning, we know. Rather, it is those things coming from a whole life and from a whole person, that persuades.

Your testimony in this trial will be transcribed. You are to read the transcript and, as individuals, or as a group, in whatever way you feel appropriate, to devise a plan to broadcast this testimony, to promulgate it and to make it known. And you are to show some concrete first step in achieving that plan. . . .

I will say that I am honored to be part of this system in which this jury has labored, because I know your sincerity and I know the difficulty of your task. And I'm also honored to be in the presence of members of this race who live their lives as the defendants here do.

We were stunned. The jury found us guilty of just one charge, trespassing. We had seen the court reporter's tears as we gave our testimony but had no idea of the impact of our stories on Judge Gomez. Our actions continued over the years, and most of us did spend some time in jail.

Our actions came from our caring—for our families, our children, our planet, and our global family as well. As a result of our group's commitment, others became involved. We "grew" social capital. Through these actions I have felt the spirit in our commitment.

The Spirit in Commitment

Spirituality is like the flu. Some get it; some don't. "They just don't get it!" is an oft-spoken phrase, but just what does it mean? Most of us refer to "getting it" as consciousness, being aware, and "in touch." To paraphrase Carl Jung, if a person lives an unconscious life, the soul dies. The soul lives only by virtue of consciousness. Spirituality in commitment is manifested in the dynamic of our inner climb.

When we merge awareness and action in our climbs, we often experience a personal transcendence. "Flow" is the holistic sensation that results from our total involvement in an activity. When we are encompassed fully in this process, our self-consciousness falls away and we become a part of something greater. At these moments I feel a oneness with all that is. Words fall away. I like to think that when our inner climbs engage our spirits so fully, so vitally, we can experience the same intrinsic rewards and sense of flow that we experience in our outer climbs.

I spoke earlier about the spirit in place. John Muir said, "The clearest way into the Universe is through a forest wilderness." And the clearest way to our own universal bedrock is through our wilderness within.

I cannot help but wonder whether, if we can continue to grow spiritually, we can create a psychology of hope. Many cynics would say, "Not in this lifetime!" But I would answer that by saying, "It has already happened."

In the 1940s the world stood witness to the greatest altruistic act of all time, a story of public commitment, a story of the greatness of humanity. During the German occupation of Denmark in 1943, the Danes learned that the Germans had planned an "Aktion" to deport all Jews to concentration camps. During a period of a few weeks in October 1943, 7,220 Jews left Denmark for Sweden, the government of which had offered them sanctuary. The Danes rented fishing boats to transport the Jews and provided loans or financial gifts to people fleeing. Danes from all walks of society came forth to help—from fishermen and taxi drivers to highly placed government officials. Even the Danish police came to help, and the Coast Guard acted as escort.

As a result, more than ninety percent of the Jews in Denmark escaped deportation to Nazi concentration camps. Of the 464 Jews who were deported from Denmark to Theresienstadt, a "model" concentration camp, only 11 died.

When asked about this remarkable feat, the Danes explained that they were only "treating their neighbors as neighbors are to be treated." The Danes always regarded the "Jewish question" as a Danish concern. Even the king wore a yellow star, the symbol imposed by Nazis to stigmatize the Jews.

When questioned about their strength in caring for the Jews, several Danes commented that it is not that the Jews owed anyone gratitude but rather what is owed through mutual friendship. Survivor Elie Weisel said of those times that some people—Danes and others—climbed to the summit of humanity by simply remaining human.

This act did not occur because the Danes have some special gene. The story is powerful because it reminds us of how often we are bystanders in life, feeling empty in a sea of possibilities. We have the same capacity in us today, and the Danish Jewry story reminds us that we can't do it alone.

This book is about a new ethos of commitment, commitment as an alive, interactive process. This new ethos will carry us toward honoring our integrity and, at the same time, will connect us from that core place of genuine caring.

We carry our climbs in our hearts; they go with us. As each of us climbs, we face more of our inner truth; we go deeper as we move toward the inaccessible summit. The higher we go, the more that is demanded of us. Through the years I have found I prefer to move steadily and slowly up the mountains, leaving the intensity-filled technical climbing for the young ones. To live life as a climb—to risk, to face fears, to trust, to ask for support, to endure, to face the crux, and to make the crucial choice beyond—all lead to embracing the spirit within. We can thus ignite our natural caring to develop conscious commitments.

The Bedrock Within

Here in the mountain kingdom of Tibet, I cannot separate my-self from the rest. The rock lives, and the clay breathes. Here I know I am spirit; here I "get" it—that we are all a part of the whole. Here I can know most clearly my own truth; I stay with myself with each breath. Yet it is so difficult to hold on to myself when I am back home. Here I experience what Socrates meant when he said, "May the inward and outward be as one."

In Tibet, I was in touch with bedrock, the solid rock that underlies loose material, the solid rock that is the very basis, the foundation, the core, of my being. May Sarton once said, "It always comes down to the same necessity. Go down deep enough, and there is always a bedrock or truth, how-ever hard." To climb higher, I had to learn to go deeper, to take more risks, to make conscious commitments. Here I fully realize it is not commitment we seek, but rather the bedrock within us. As we continue to climb with intention, hope, and imagination, we can climb toward the summit of our true selves. Thus we open the doors to the invisible—through lives of commitment and caring that shape posterity.

Recommended Reading

Interested readers may enjoy some of the books that have shaped my thinking:

Ahrons, Constance. *The Good Divorce: Keeping Your Family Together When Your Marriage Comes Apart.* New York: HarperCollins. 1994.

Berenbaum, Michael. *The World Must Know.* New York: Little, Brown and Company, 1993.

Block, Gay, and Malka Drucker. *Rescuers: Portraits of Moral Courage in the Holocaust.* New York: Holmes and Meier, 1992.

Bly, Robert. *The Sibling Society.* Reading, MA.: Addison-Wesley, 1996.

Borysenko, Joan. *Minding the Body, Mending the Mind.* New York: Bantam Books, 1988.

Carter, Betty, and Joan K. Peters. *Love, Honor and Negotiate.* New York: Simon and Schuster, 1996.

Daumal, Rene. *Mt. Analogue: A Non-Euclidean Adventure in Mountain Climbing.* Baltimore: Penguin, 1974.

David-Neel, Alexandra. *My Journey to Lhasa.* Boston: Beacon Press, 1992.

Edelman, Marion. *The Measure of Our Success.* New York: HarperPerennial, 1993.

Goleman, Daniel. *Emotional Intelligence.* New York: Harper-Collins, 1996.

Kabat-Zinn, Jon. *Wherever You Go There You Are.* New York: Hyperion, 1994.

Lawrence, Andrea Mead, and Sara Burnaby. *A Practice of Mountains.* New York: Seabury Press, 1980.

Leider, Richard and David Shapiro. *Repacking Your Bags.* San Francisco: Berrett-Koehler, 1996.

Lerner, Harriet. *Live Savers.* New York: HarperCollins, 1996.

Morrison, Toni. *Song of Solomon.* New York: Plume, 1987.

Richo, David. *How to Be an Adult.* New York: Paulist Press, 1991.

Rubin, Lillian. *The Transcendent Child.* New York: Harper-Collins, 1996.

Silverstein, Olga. *The Courage to Raise Good Men.* New York: Viking, 1995.

Whyte, David. *The Heart Aroused.* New York: Doubleday, 1994.

Zukav, Gary. *The Seat of the Soul.* New York: Simon and Schuster, 1990.